NATURE'S SUBLIME

NATURE'S SUBLIME

An Essay in Aesthetic Naturalism

Robert S. Corrington

LEXINGTON BOOKS
Lanham • Boulder • New York • Toronto • Plymouth, UK

Published by Lexington Books
A wholly owned subsidiary of The Rowman & Littlefield Publishing Group,
Inc.
4501 Forbes Boulevard, Suite 200, Lanham, Maryland 20706
www.rowman.com

10 Thornbury Road, Plymouth PL6 7PP, United Kingdom

British Library Cataloguing in Publication Information Available

Library of Congress Cataloging-in-Publication Data

Library of Congress Cataloging-in-Publication Data Available
ISBN 978-0-7391-8213-0 (cloth : alk. paper)—ISBN 978-0-7391-8214-7 (electronic)

℗™ The paper used in this publication meets the minimum requirements of
American National Standard for Information Sciences Permanence of Paper
for Printed Library Materials, ANSI/NISO Z39.48-1992.

Printed in the United States of America

DEDICATED TO
ROBERT C. NEVILLE

Der Zeit ihre Kunst,
Der Kunst ihre Freiheit
(Art for the Times, Freedom for Art)
Creed of the Viennese Secessionist Movement 1898

CONTENTS

PREFACE

In this book I have ventured into new territory and have further developed the method of ordinal phenomenology from my earlier books as the primary means of access to the traits of self, community, religious phenomena, and the domains of art and the aesthetic. In addition, I have continued to radicalize classical psychoanalysis through an ordinal regrounding that renders it more capacious and correlated to the orders of nature and nature's unconscious. This has entailed taking issue with specific theories and thinkers such as Husserl, Heidegger, and Marion in phenomenology and Freud, Jung, Rank, Reich, Kohut, and Kristeva in psychoanalysis, both critically and appreciatively. Ordinal phenomenology critiques both transcendental and hermeneutic phenomenology as resting on an implied and inadequate metaphysics that leads to a near obsession with certainty and the evident, via essentialization. Ordinal psychoanalysis critiques the drive theory of Freud from the standpoint of Kohut's self theory as enriched by other post-Freudian perspectives, which are themselves reconstructed from an ordinal perspective.

The concept of selving is one of the key motifs of the text as it appears in both personal and communal forms. It is complex and vast in its various modes of being and cannot be reduced to a cluster of essences that somehow prescind from the often unruly orders of the world. Selving, involving the full force of the unconscious in its threefold reality—the unconscious of nature, the collective unconscious, and the personal unconscious—is highly resistant to traditional forms of phenomenological description and requires an ordinal treatment that probes into its most regnant and important ordinal locations, however resistant to description they may appear to be at first glance. Ordinal analyses and descriptions bring out the full scope and richness of the selving process.

Communal semiotics further impacts on the selving process and the self/community correlation is ripe with momenta that are phenomenologically available through a kind of semiotics of infinity or infinitizing. The actual infinite of signs and interpretants, that is, new signs, gives life and embodiment to the nascent self as it begins its journey among the signs of its communities. The self belongs to more communities than it knows and part of the struggle of existence is to find some coherence among these communities and their often competing value schemes.

Among the most powerful signs and interpretants are those of religion and art and the boundary between these two great dimensions of life are often hard to draw. However, with care it is possible to demarcate the correlation between the religious use of a sign or object and its aesthetic use. This book argues that the sphere of art is more important and salvific for the selving process, personal and communal, than that of religion. Among the several reasons for this two stand out: (1) art is less tribal and more universal than religion; and (2) religion and religious identity have a built-in (hard-wired) tendency toward violence while art does not.

The most fundamental distinction within the one nature that there is, namely, that between *nature naturing* and *nature natured*, permeates the entire framework. *Nature naturing* can be defined as, "nature perennially creating itself out of itself alone," while *nature natured* can be defined as, "the innumerable orders of the world," which have no collective outer shape or contour.

My argument is that this primal distinction is best preserved and articulated in an *aesthetic naturalism* that serves as the metaphysical horizon for this book. The perspective is fully *naturalistic* in that it affirms that nature is all that there is and that there is no such thing as a supernatural realm. This naturalism is *aesthetic* because it affirms the primacy of beauty and the sublime in any capacious metaphysics that probes into the deepest dimensions of *nature naturing* as they become relevant to *nature natured*. The terminology of "ordinal metaphysics" is used when the stress is on the innumerable orders of *nature natured*, making it a part of the larger metaphysics of aesthetic naturalism.

Robert S. Corrington
Drew University

INTRODUCTION

In foundational level philosophy it is profoundly difficult to extricate method from the matter being thought through, precisely because method and its matter are co-given on the deepest layers of encounter. One does not simply choose a method from a warehouse of stand-alone methods that can be applied in a neutral way to this or that complex or order within nature. Rather, the process is more akin to creating a work of art in which the media and the product shape and challenge each other in the process of contrivance. Method and its 'objective' correlate go all the way down.

Yet it is also the case that some methods are better than others for particular tasks and that a judicious choice at the outset of philosophic exploration and query can make the difference between a fecund and powerful portrayal of nature and a sterile and truncated caricature of the world and its innumerable orders. The first question is: what is being asked about in this essay? That is, what is the 'matter' of thought for which the right method is being sought? The answer is that this essay is concerned with seeking the primary traits within nature of the human process, the nature of human communities, the structure and powers of religion, and the powers and potencies of art. These four dimensions of the world, this fourfold, as parts of nature, are explored in a methodic

I

way through a novel use of a method that has had a long and positive standing in philosophy since the nineteenth century; namely, phenomenology. However, classical phenomenology rests on dubious and weak metaphysical presuppositions that must be reconstructed if it is to function in this treatise as the primary method of query and description.

Here we shall see that classical phenomenology in Husserl and Heidegger, rests on inadequate ontological principles and categories showing that the correlation of method and subject matter goes deep. Our second question thus is: Insofar as phenomenology is the method chosen in this work can it be reconfigured to better correlate with its generic subject matter; namely, self, community, religion, and art? And if so, may we envision a new way of seeing the relationship between metaphysics and phenomenology?

The term "metaphysics" has several meanings in the tradition and we must be clear which is being used here. What is *not* being meant here is the idea of a separate realm beyond the physical or a supernatural order that may or may not intersect with nature itself. Rather, the term "metaphysics" refers to the study and articulation of the most pervasive traits of the one nature that there is. For Dewey metaphysics is the study of the "generic traits of existence," while for Buchler it is the exploration of "whatever is in whatever way it is. And for aesthetic naturalism metaphysics is the analysis of the potencies of *nature naturing* and of the innumerable orders of *nature natured* (or "creation" in a monotheism). And in none of these latter cases is metaphysics involved with a search for an extra-natural first cause or an external omnipotent power.

In what follows both phenomenology as method, and metaphysics as subject matter, will be reconstructed. An *ordinal* phenomenology will replace both transcendental and hermeneutical phenomenology, while an aesthetic naturalist metaphysics will both guide and be shaped by ordinal phenomenology. Again, it is impossible to find a 'pure' method that is applied to a 'pure' subject matter. However, the process is not a purely arbitrary or subjective one but has many ways of showing its intersubjective and (reasonably) objective power.

In addition to introducing the novel method of ordinal phenomenology, this treatise develops a rethinking of psychoanalysis as the conceptual *medium* through which we are to understand the human process and its embeddedness in community, its religions, and the realms of artistic creation and assimilation. What is called for is an *ordinal* psychoanalysis that challenges the narcissism of classical Freudian metapsychology and remains in dialogue with Jung, Rank, Kohut, and Kristeva as it develops a self-psychoanalysis rooted metaphysically in the *selving* process.

What this means is that the method of ordinal phenomenology will struggle to describe the generic traits of nature with as much openness to the 'way' and 'how' of nature as this finitely located process can provide. At the same time ordinal psychoanalysis will struggle to illuminate the rhythms of the unconscious as they directly impinge on the shaping and unfolding of meanings in the intra-psychic and inter-psychic spheres. One of the most striking aspects of this dual approach will be the phenomenology of the unconscious of nature and of the human unconscious that is rooted in nature's unconscious.

When dealing with the unconscious we seem to come up against an abyss that forces phenomenology to come to a halt. But this is not quite so. Jung forcefully argued that while one can never (phenomenologically) see an archetype, one could see the innumerable archetypal images that were caused by it. His argument was a mixture of an empirical induction on one side with a Kantian transcendental argument on the other. The latter move is the important one here. Peirce called this strategy an 'abductive' argument whereby you go from an instance under study to a rule that explains it. A transcendental/abductive argument goes from the conditions of the observed to the positing of a cause behind the scenes that must be there to explain the fact that is observed. Hence, for Jung, an archetype must exist to explain why archetypal images are so universal around the world, in dream material, art, religion, and psychopathology.

The most exciting and demanding philosophic work takes place where phenomenological description is compelled to confront a specific transcendental argument. The ultimate goal would be to convert all transcendental/abductive arguments into direct phenomenological descriptions where the archetype, say, is seen *an sich.* Should ordinal phenomenology accept its limits at the outset and honor the abyss that it can't cross, leaving it to the abductive leap to posit something that can't be directly intuited? Or should the practitioner of ordinal phenomenology push against the limits of this method of all methods hoping to get closer and closer to the phenomenon as it is in itself? Or is it the case that there is no way to answer these two questions in advance and on a strategic level, while there might be some give and take on the pragmatic and tactic level? This essay will argue for the notion that there are *pragmatic* a prioris that can shape and direct experience and which function *as if* they are knowable and just beyond experience, but only just.

The issue of the potencies, rooted in the heart of *nature naturing,* is especially problematic for ordinal phenomenology. We can experience their effects within the orders of *nature natured* as manifest in an influx of power and meaning within given orders of relevance, orders that stand out in sharp contrast from a less intense background of quotidian reality. In religious and aesthetic language, the potencies are encountered as *sacred folds,* that is, as intensified semiotic fields that fold in on themselves over and over again increasing the depth and power of meaning with each infolding. The core of the sacred fold is its rootedness in the

unconscious of nature as channeled through the unconscious of
the human self. Within the unconscious depths of the sacred fold
is the archetype that preserves and protects the conjunction of
power and meaning for that specific fold and its foldings.

The intimate correlation of phenomenology and metaphysics is
secured in the ordinal perspective that grounds both method and
the nature that method serves to disclose. Ordinal phenomenology is the 'how' for unfolding the 'way' of nature's orders and
nature's orders are the given and co-given for ordinal phenomenology. What then is *ordinal* phenomenology and what are the
metaphysical principles that occur with it and why are they chosen rather than any others? How does ordinal phenomenology
differ from Husserl's transcendental phenomenology and Heidegger's hermeneutic phenomenology?

Traditionally phenomenology has been envisioned as the foundational method of methods, a first philosophy, which is metaphysically neutral. It is a careful and painstaking process of drop-
ping away one metaphysical presupposition after another so that
the pure phenomenality of the phenomenon can begin to shine
forth in its own right as made possible through a series of directed
and intentional mental acts that rotate the phenomenon through
different perceptual horizons until it has been seen in its essential
features. Classical phenomenology is not quite an epistemology
nor a gestalt psychology but is a unique approach to the phenomena held to be of intense interest to philosophy in its most generic
sense.

The goal of classical phenomenology, both transcendental and
hermeneutic, is to isolate and then describe the essence of the
phenomenon under investigation. There is a special series of intentional acts by means of which the inessential is stripped away
thereby allowing the essence or essences to become evident to
phenomenological circumspection. The essence occupies a special ontological niche, vaguely Platonic in its ideality. To find this

essence the phenomenologist must adumbrate (shadow and rotate) the phenomenon through its various modes of self-showing
so that the vagaries of its merely empirical modalities are let go so
that its quasi-eternal essence is brought into, or allowed into, the
attentive consciousness of the phenomenologist. With the showing and describing of essence (*Wesensschau*) the task of phenomenology is complete.

In transcendental phenomenology the focus is on the a priori
acts of the universal depth structures of the transcendental ego
that sends out, as it were, a series of intentional acts that surround
and lift up the phenomenon to make it available to a seizure of its
essentializing core. In hermeneutic phenomenology the focus is
on the whole phenomenal field in which the human process is
part of an interpretive nexus that lights up the World within
which phenomena disclose their essential traits. Heidegger states
this difference in 1927 just after publishing his *Sein und Zeit*:

> *For Husserl* the phenomenological reduction, which he
> worked out for the first time expressly in the *Ideas Toward a
> Pure Phenomenology and Phenomenological Philosophy*
> (1913), is the method of leading phenomenological vision from
> the natural attitude of the human being whose life is involved
> in the world of things and persons back to the transcendental
> life of consciousness and its noetic-noematic experiences, in
> which objects are constituted as correlates of consciousness.
> *For us*, phenomenological reduction means leading pheno-
> menological vision back from the apprehension of a being,
> whatever may be the character of that apprehension, to the
> understanding of the being of this being (projecting upon the
> way it is unconcealed). (Heidegger 1927: 21)

Heidegger captures the different foci that animate and direct
transcendental and hermeneutic phenomenology. Husserl's
transcendental version of phenomenology works through the no-
etic acts of transcendental consciousness as they shape the noe-

matic content giving rise to clear and distinct phenomena that are ready to reveal their essential traits to a concise thematic awareness. The certainty of the evident is the goal of this kind of phenomenology. Heidegger's phenomenological problematic moves boldly (in his early philosophy) into the ontological difference between Being and the thing in being seeking the unhiddenness of each side of this perennial divide. Further, Heidegger drives below the transcendental ego to the more primordial phenomenon of the *Dasein* that is the clearing within which and as which being-in-the-world as a totality becomes the opening onto the innumerable orders of *nature natured*. The self-showing of the phenomenon is lit up and brought to a phenomenal clearing through temporality where the disclosure of essence loses some of the Platonic features still operative in transcendental phenomenology.

What then is ordinal phenomenology and what difference does it make methodologically and what metaphysical commitments does it require in order to fulfill its task of rendering the traits of World and nature intelligible? Nonordinal phenomenology remains tied to an atemporal Platonism or, in its hermeneutic form, an essentiality that is historical but still essentializing through and through.

Again it must be noted that there is no 'pure' phenomenology free from metaphysical commitments. What is being sought is a metaphysics that best serves the needs and task of phenomenology. Its task is to bring into thematic awareness the most fundamental traits of nature and the World (worldhood) so that experience can be opened to the most generic clearing obtainable by the finite human process (selving). For aesthetic naturalism, the principles of ordinality are held to be the most generic and powerful for metaphysics in general and for the thematization of ordinal phenomenology in particular.

The first substitution to be made is that the word and concept of "essence" is to be replaced by the word and concept of "trait," where the latter term has a striking metaphysical neutrality. Anything whatsoever is a trait while only certain traits are held to be essences. The ordinal perspective does not rely on or use a concept of essence and prefers to speak of "traits of an enduring quality in certain respects in certain orders," rather than speak bluntly of some kind of universal trans-ordinal essence. Ordinal theory denies that trans-ordinal essences exist and that what transcendental and hermeneutic phenomenologies describe as essences are, again, traits demarcated because they have a certain enduring quality in a certain respect. But the metaphysical concept of essences is both imperial and inept. It is imperial in that it ends up, unbeknownst to itself, imposing a static trait or trait cluster onto the sheer ordinal complexity of the order(s) under investigation. This colonizes the other traits of the pertinent order and renders them into a subaltern status. It is inept in that it mishandles the ambiguous and divergent traits that happen to fall just outside of its essentializing purview.

By shifting to the metaphysical concept of traits phenomenology can gain an elasticity that enables it to slowly enter into the complex inner and outer dynamics of the complexes it seeks to describe. While some traits may be privileged for certain purposes it does not follow that they are more real in a metaphysical hierarchy, only more pertinent within a specific mode of phenomenological inquiry. Some traits will have more scope and some will be more fleeting but neither will be more essential in all respects. The concept of essence is a pragmatic and tactical one not a constitutive one, that is, an essence is posited for a specific short or long termed practical goal where it is desirable to have one trait accentuated over others.

Ordinal phenomenology seeks to isolate and describe those traits that are relevant and pertinent to the human orders and the nature within which these orders obtain. The ordinal perspective exists as a metaphysical perspective that functions prior to phenomenology itself. That is, phenomenology, contrary to its occasional polemical claims, is not pre-metaphysical, but always operates within a, for the most part, unexamined metaphysical perspective. Essentialism is roughly Platonic and at least operates as a quest for certainty (Dewey 1929). The *Evident* is what it is because essences are held to be clear and distinct universals at the heart of intentional acts of consciousness that deliver the essence(s) to thematic awareness.

For aesthetic naturalism, ordinal metaphysics is the most powerful framework for regrounding and reshaping the task and goals of phenomenology. Trait language is the closest language we have to metaphysical inclusiveness. By seeing everything in nature as a trait or as an order of traits all metaphysical hierarchies are dissolved in one stroke. There is no such thing as *the* trait of traits or *the* order of orders, only innumerable traits that prevail in innumerable ways and phenomenology has the task of tracing out those traits that it deems important for a particular human personal and/or communal need.

The concept of ordinality is fundamental and applies to both method and subject matter; that is, to the *way* of phenomenology and to the *what* of nature. It also shapes and deepens the scope and penetrating/inviting power of the medium of psychoanalysis by locating it within the rhythms of the entire embedded selving process with its many religious and aesthetic sacred folds. Ordinal psychoanalysis is open to the innumerable ways in which the selving process transacts with the deepest pulsations of *nature naturing*.

Originally developed by Justus Buchler (Buchler 1966; 1990) the principle of ordinality is extremely capacious while at the same time providing sharp tools for making careful and precise distinctions; that is, for framing genuine, not paper, differences.

For the ordinal perspective nature is understood to be constituted by innumerable natural complexes, although the word "natural" is not strictly necessary as there are no non-natural orders. The phrase "natural complex" is used to remind us that nature is ubiquitous and that whatever there is, in whatever mode it is, or in whatever sphere it is, it is fully and always a part of the one nature that there is. Everything that we can point to, imagine, think, bump into, long for, hate, desire, flee from, ignore, devour, abject, destroy, give birth to, or in any way alter, is a natural complex. There are no simples in nature; as such a complex would have to have no relations and no internal traits, an impossibility. Hartshorne posited simples through his principle of contrasts: if complex occasions exist then simples must be their contrast reality. But this does not follow logically or in any other way. Complexity goes all the way down.

Once it is established that nature is constituted by natural complexes and that there are no simples, it follows that each complex has 'internal' traits. As above, the concept of essence plays only a tactical role in an ordinal metaphysics. We may call a trait or a trait-cluster an essence if we need to highlight it for specific personal or communal purposes. But this is a process that can tear a trait out of its ordinal context and magnify it beyond its actual scope and instantiation. In extreme cases this becomes a form of psychopathology in which the trait is over read and becomes part of a paranoid delusional semiotic system.

Thus at the 'low' end of the given natural complex we have an order with its own 'inner' or subaltern traits, none of which are simple. Idealistic systems, especially the process variety, assume that each trait within an order, say, an actual occasion, is in relation with every other trait 'within' that order. But that does not follow. From the ordinal perspective no one trait will be related to every other and each trait will have only partial relations with the innumerable others that obtain in the natural complex. This is so for two reasons: (1) within the natural complex there are an infinite number of relations, that is of traits; and (2) there are an infinite number of 'external' relations of varying kinds between the natural complex and other orders of nature. Note, that I did not say that external relations were with *all* of the other orders of nature, but only with *other* orders.

Strictly, the distinction between internal and external relations does not function within the ordinal framework as it is too simplistic and it envisions a web of total connectivity wherein all orders are internally (epistemically and literally) known to each other in a vast total super order, or via an underground extensive continuum. Thus at the 'high' end we have the idea that nature is a vast totality, a unified order of all orders, a coherent system of all systems in which each constituent is internally/mentally related to each other. The glue for the vast internal system of systems is usually a version of panpsychism; for Peirce, Whitehead, and Hartshorne, the idea that so-called matter is a form of condensed mind. Once the universe/nature is mentalized it becomes much easier to believe in the idea of a total super order of traits all bound together by a living awareness, that, while primitive in lower inorganic orders, is just conscious enough to provide relational connection across the board. One of the most dangerous effects of panpsychism is that it silently abjects nature's unruly unconscious and cuts thought off from the abyss (*Ungrund*) that is the ultimate fore-having for thought.

For some like Royce nature is an infinite self-representative series in which each member of the series perfectly mirrors the other members of the series—an actual infinite. Or, coming at it from the other end, nature is seen as a transcendental representation within the synthesis of the transcendental imagination as it imposes temporality and space onto an unknown manifold—as in Heidegger's regrounding of Kant's *First Critique* (Heidegger 1929) in its more daring first edition.

Just as there is no rock bottom simple, and that there is no present or final super order, as longed for by Peirce, so too there is no extra-natural divine order that oversees what takes place within the one nature that there is. Aesthetic naturalism rejects both the classical god of theism and the halfway god of panentheism, the former being ruled out in principle as incompatible with the principle of ordinality, while the latter, in spite of its often brilliant articulation and defense, softening the edges of nature and still clinging to the doctrine of internal relation and a muted eschatology. Aesthetic naturalism has a very limited role for eschatology as a needed goad for personal and social transformation but in consort with evolutionary awareness it rejects the idea that history per se has been, is, or will be in any sense purposive. Whether in the mode of Christian *Heilsgeschichte* or Heidegger's *Seinsgeschichte*, the longing for a (largely) determined history of histories flourishes where a broken metaphysics weds itself to human pathological need. There are innumerable histories but only the one nature that there is. Histories are local and tribal and usually conflict with each other. Histories tend to be self-serving and dyadic with reasonably clear demarcations between the inner and outer members of the tribe. It is part of the inner logic of self-encapsulated histories to become violent at some stage of development.

For some, metaphysics itself, as the expression of onto-theology, is violent in its very nature insofar as it posits a highest being and further imposes a closed set of genera on the flux of becoming that is the really real in and as nature. Metaphysics is, of course, defined in a rather mechanical and predictable way as totalizing phallic/masculine machinery that kills the creativity and novelty of a becoming and always fluid universe. The highest being is held to have produced nature or the universe through the principle of sufficient reason (Leibniz), which argues that there must be a rational cause for everything that exists as well as for each item itself that exists. The world as a (bound) totality is the necessary, not random, result of a once-and-for-all creative act whereby the indeterminate becomes the determinate (Neville 1980). The transition from god to world, as posited by onto-theology (the form that metaphysics has historically taken according to this argument) is rational, complete, knowable by use of human reason, and correlates the power of god with male privilege and power.

One can make two responses to this attack on metaphysics: (1) one can argue that it is a limited and historically distorted vision of the craft of metaphysics as actually practiced; or (2) one can take the more positive approach and argue for and present a form of metaphysics that is not a form of onto-theology and hence not subject to its critique. The second response is the one to be pursued here as it moves more quickly to the heart of the matter and shows that the ordinal perspective is neither onto-theology nor does it collapse into its alleged opposite; namely, a realm of sheer becoming with no generic features.

Ordinal metaphysics is clearly not a form of onto-theology insofar as it has no place for a highest natural complex (order) that stands outside of nature as some kind of creative generative source, nor does the ordinal perspective have a closed set of genera that stand in a hierarchy of being with the lowest genus having less being than the highest. For the ordinal framework there are no degrees of being. Nothing is more or less real than anything else. This follows from the principle of ontological parity, which states that nature admits no degrees of being only diverse ways or kinds of being. Ontological parity is contrasted to the principle of ontological priority, which does insist that some things are more real, more primal, or more foundational than others. Almost all philosophy, consciously or unconsciously, maintains some form of ontological priority in its stated or implied metaphysics. So one gets statements of the following varieties: objects are more real than words, or spirit is more real than matter, or matter is more real than spirit, or the Will is more real than phenomena, or sense data alone are real, or only consciousness exists, or only matter is truly real, or only ideas in the mind of god are real, or only brain states are real, and so on.

In the ordinal perspective one always says: X is real in just the way that it is real and is never more or less real than Y. The stone faces on Mt. Rushmore are not more real than my passing thought that I want to eat ice cream, only differently real. Neither natural complex is the paradigm for the "really real," even though many philosophies will privilege the former as being somehow more metaphysically substantive. For surely granite is extremely hard and durable and has more being than a thought that flashes across the brain and its attendant consciousness but then disappears as quickly as it came. But why assume that granite is more real than a thought? Each complex has traits and each stands in relation to other complexes and has 'internal' traits that ramify indefinitely. Each prevails in nature in the distinctive ways that it does prevail and each is subject to human appraisal and analysis. For the ordinal perspective there is no such thing as a privileged order or complex that is paradigmatic for all other orders. In the words of Justus Buchler:

> Now along with the notion of a complex as "unreal" we must discard the notion of some complexes as "less" and other complexes as "more" real. Let us contrast a principle of ontological priority—which has flourished from Parmenides to Whitehead and Heidegger, and which continues to flourish in unexpected ways—with a principle of ontological parity. In terms of the latter, whatever is discriminated in any way (whether it is "encountered" or produced or otherwise related to) is a natural complex, and no complex is more "real," more "natural," more "genuine," or more "ultimate," than any other. (Buchler 1966; 1990: 30–31)

Further, the insistence on parity also compels ordinal phenomenology to focus on all discriminanda, that is, all differences, great or small, and not to efface them as somehow being unimportant: "The principle of parity obliges us to receive and accept all discriminanda" (Buchler 1966; 1990: 33). Put differently, the practice of ontological parity heightens the philosophical senses to the sheer prevalence of all traits and their subalterns within their respective phenomenological horizons.

The radicality of this aspect of the ordinal perspective needs to be reinforced. Once one accepts the principle of ontological parity, the entire onto-theological system collapses. However, this collapse need not entail a postmodern rejection of all forms of metaphysics. On the contrary, it prepares the clearing for the ordinal reconstruction of metaphysics in attunement with the requirements and demands of ontological parity. On a much deeper level the spiritual practice of ontological parity calls for a mindfulness that changes the very practice of philosophy. There is a striking parallel between Buchler's notion of query and the sense of parity, and Heidegger's mode of mindful attunement as expressed in his private notes from the Nazi period:

> Mindfulness is attuning of the grounding-attunement of man insofar as this attunement attunes him unto be-ing and unto the groundership of the truth of be-ing. . . . This grounding projecting-opening en-thinks the truth of be-ing and—however different and contrary this may seem—is thereby nonetheless en-owned only by be-ing itself. (Heidegger 1938–1939: 40–41)

The human process (selving) opens itself to the offering of be-ing and grounds itself in this offering so that it can fulfill its own excellence as the place of be-ing's approach, however fitful under the conditions of its historical withdrawal. Buchler rejects any sense of a destiny of being but retains a sense of a transformation of the self through its open permeability to the vast vistas enabled by the liberating power of ontological parity, vistas that bring with them a heightened form of mindfulness.

Husserl, less strikingly, employs the tactic of bracketing, or reduction, in which the phenomenologist steps back from making any existential claims about the existence or existential status of the phenomenon being investigated, especially about any metaphysical claims that transcend its immediate data. This frees phenomenological description to become open to a larger area of phenomena and deprivileges static spatio-temporal medium sized objects so that one can, for example, describe emotions without asking about their existential or ontological status: "everything transcendent that is involved must be bracketed, or be assigned the index of indifference, of epistemological nullity, an index which indicates; the existence of all these transcendencies, whether I believe in them or not, is not here my concern; this is not the place to make judgments about them; they are entirely irrelevant" (Husserl 1907: 31). Phenomenology thus lets go of making existential claims about the ontological status of its chosen phenomena and confines itself to their description and their particular modes of self-givenness.

The principle of ontological parity is an even stronger framework or tool that one can bring to phenomenological description in that it makes it possible to examine and describe *any* type of natural complex that is humanly available to phenomenological appraisal. It has a much more sophisticated understanding of the given and its relationship with the co-given and a more tolerant attitude to the nature of the evident (*Evidenz*). The ongoing and continually renewed commitment to ontological parity is like a spiritual practice that infuses ordinal phenomenology with a radical openness to the rich and unending complexity of phenomena (natural complexes) in nature.

How does this commitment to ontological parity work in the practice of ordinal phenomenology? The first thing to note is that it is profoundly difficult to overcome the innumerable temptations to impose some kind of ontological priority onto the experiential fields described and rendered available by phenomenology. The very doing of phenomenology, as the science and art of the description of the key natural complexes that are open and available to conscious attention, requires a severe discipline and a level of self-consciousness that is hard to maintain for any extended period of time. Priority commitments easily slip into the choices phenomenologists make, especially if the goal remains that of essentialization in the Husserlian sense. Paradigms emerge that act like gravitational masses pulling and distorting the phenomenal data so that priority schema quickly take over and erect small or large order ontological hierarchies that push any number of important traits into the penumbra of vision. Habit and laziness serve to reinforce and reward priority schemes and to block out the light of the more tenuous or delicate traits that should have an equal place within the resultant phenomenal field.

Ordinal phenomenology is what it is because of its commitment to ontological parity. Here the fate of the phenomenon under investigation is very different. There is no search for some foundational *ur*-phenomenon that would ground all other phenomena within the selected region of nature. By the same token, there is no drive to find a trans-temporal or trans-ordinal essence that would be the true phenomenon underneath all modes of its semblance (Heidegger 1927). Ordinal phenomenology examines traits from a variety of perspectives, that is, it rotates the natural complex through several (or more) of its ordinal locations, and refuses to privilege one of these locations as being the foundational or "really real" thing in itself. Strictly put, the *ding an sich* is all of the phenomenon's ordinal locations, not one privileged over the others.

In fact Husserl comes close to the method of ordinal phenomenology in his 1900 *Logical Investigations VI* where he describes the process of working through a series of partial mental intentions around and about the phenomenon under investigation by phenomenological intuition:

> Objectively put: the object shows itself from a variety of sides. What was pictorially suggested from one side, becomes confirmed in full perception from another; what was merely adumbrated or given indirectly and subsidiarily as background, from one side, at least receives a portrait-sketch from another, only to appear 'just as it is' from another side. All perceiving and imagining is, on our view, a web of partial intentions, fused together in the unity of a single intention. The correlate of this last intention is the thing, while the correlate of its partial intentions are *the thing ' s parts and aspects*. Only in this way can we understand how consciousness reaches out beyond what it actually experiences. It can so to say mean beyond itself, and its meaning can be fulfilled. (Husserl 1900: 701)

In Husserl's language, consciousness links together the numerous "sketches" of the self-giving of the thing into a fuller portrait of the thing as it appears in its fulfilled meaning. In so doing, consciousness moves "beyond itself." It is this last idea that opens up the door to a more fully ordinal view. For ordinal phenomenology the full phenomenality of the phenomenon is found through the initial opening into the "variety of sides" in the immediate forms of the evident. But this adumbration process only scratches the surface and doesn't work as well for complexes that are simply not available for sense rich encounter.

Philosophers often follow common sense and build epistemologies, as noted, around garden-variety middle-sized objects with more or less physical traits, both primary (mind independent like extension) and secondary (mind dependent like color). The violence done to the portrayal of nature is clear to the ordinal scheme, which refuses to create or defend *any* paradigm that would attempt to stand duty for nature or the World (worldhood).

Simply put, there is no place for reductive epistemological or ontological paradigms in aesthetic naturalism, only the endless unfolding of the innumerable orders of nature manifest to ordinal phenomenology through traits of indefinite variety and complexity. There is no bottom and no top to the orders of nature and ordinal phenomenology has no extra-natural or extra-historical goals to pursue. Nature gives itself to ordinal phenomenology fully but only insofar as the working phenomenologist continues in the spiritual practice of ontological parity and has the patience to slowly and carefully trace out the ordinally located traits of the phenomena under investigation.

In agreement with Husserl, aesthetic naturalism affirms that nature has the modality of self-showing insofar as its traits are available for scrutiny and analysis by sign using organisms like ourselves. In 1907 Husserl asserts: "Our phenomenological sphere, the sphere of absolute clarity, of immanence in the true sense, reaches no further than self-givenness reaches" (Husserl 1907: 8). Phenomena (natural complexes) show/give themselves to the patient phenomenologist who uses the technique of ordinal analysis and the spiritual practice of ontological parity to enhance the self-manifesting of the selected orders of the world.

Jean-Luc Marion echoes Husserl's words from the above text and makes a tight correlation between bracketing (reduction) and givenness. The phenomenological reduction refuses the transcendent modalities of phenomena and insists that all phenomenological descriptions remain in the sphere of pure immanence, that is, pure givenness. His equation is simple: so much reduction to immanence so much givenness. The reduction, as noted, is a weaker version of ontological parity, but it helps phenomenology part way down the road by upgrading more elusive and marginal phenomena:

> The reduction thus operates like a sort of middleman who leads the visible toward givenness; it leads scattered, potential,

confused, and uncertain visibles (mere appearances, outlines, impressions, vague intuitions, supposed facts, opinions, "absurd theories," etc.) to givenness, according to their degree of phenomenality. The reduction measures the level of givenness in each appearance so as to establish its right to appear or not. (Marion 1997: 15)

The reduction to immanence insures that elusive and subaltern traits become part of the panoply of the given, of the gifting of the phenomena to phenomenological intuition. Existence claims are muted and the sheer givenness of all available traits governs the tasks of description. However, the classical approach, even as enriched in important ways by Marion, still clings to the idea that there may be a phenomenal trait that won't "establish its right to appear" to enlightened intuition. Even with a more capacious ontology, pre-ordinal phenomenologies will have some form of ontological priority within their operative (pre-thematized) ontology. This is one of the reasons why the ongoing commitment to and practice of ontological parity is so important—it is, as can't be noted enough, a key to the full liberation of phenomenology as an emancipated method as allied to a metaphysics that lets nature be the fullness that it is.

Metaphysically and phenomenologically we can say that a given complex/order prevails in more orders than can ever be fully known or completely explored. This gives a sense of humility to the practice of phenomenology. An example of ordinal exploration attuned to a sense of ontological parity will help. We start with the proverbial "cat on the mat," a favored example of some analytic philosophers who prefer Spartan ontologies to add an artificial crispness to their corresponding Spartan epistemologies. But we immediately complicate the phenomenological picture by having not one but two cats, and by having them being fully mobile within their species-specific environment (*Umwelt*).

The single cat on the mat can be easily described through a quick series of profiles of its physical appearance. Its environment is limited to the rug upon which it sits and since it is not doing anything there is no need to bring in temporal descriptions or qualifiers. You might catch a yawn but otherwise phenomenological description proceeds without leaving the immediacy of the present spatio-temporal cat/mat configuration. Epistemologically one can debate whether it is better to claim that the cat on the mat is a sense datum or that it is a physical object causing the sense datum. For phenomenology, that decision doesn't have any pragmatic value as its descriptions continue regardless. At the end of the day all you have is a singular cat occupying a singular space-time order.

Ordinal phenomenology proceeds in a radically different way and quickly breaks free from the tyranny of the static spatio-temporal visual paradigm. The physical cat, in this case, cats, will still be a part of phenomenological description but no longer the only or the most important order of analysis and description. We will end up a long way from the cat on the mat, yet, in another sense, even closer than that cat/mat complex. While transcendental phenomenology privileges the immediacy of the *Evident* (*Evidenz*), and stresses the primacy of the visual field, ordinal phe– nomenology relies on all of the senses and has room for the ambiguous, the partial, and the incomplete. To over stress the *Evident* is to load the process too much on the side of certainty—a certainty that can be had, but only by narrowing the phenomenal field to a fraction of its actual breadth. And it is to cling to the physical aspect of phenomena, as that seems most available and reliable.

On the other hand, hermeneutic phenomenology makes a sharp distinction between the "ontic" and the "ontological" with the former term denoting the empirical and inductive and the latter term denoting the 'properly' philosophical essences that are known phenomenologically. There is an almost puritanical obsession with keeping merely ontic knowledge out of hermeneutic phenomenology. Yet Heidegger also acknowledges that ontology and phenomenology must co-establish each other if either is to become complete: "Phenomenology is the way of access to, and the demonstrative manner of determination of, that which is to become the theme of ontology. *Ontology is possible only as phenomenology*. The phenomenological concept of phenomenon, as self-showing, means the being of being" (Heidegger 1927a: 33). The current perspective concurs with Heidegger's affirmation of the correlation of subject and method, but with two qualifications: (1) he limits ontology to the existential analytic of *Dasein* rather than tying it to a much larger ordinal-type metaphysics of nature beyond and around *Dasein*; and (2) the Being *(Sein)* problematic itself must be transposed to the place where it encounters the dark fissuring between *nature naturing* and *nature natured*, which is deeper down in reality than the polarity of Being/Nonbeing.

Thus, again, for ordinal phenomenology the distinction between the ontic and the ontological is too rigid and must be used, if at all, pragmatically. That is, there are traits within the phenomena that are local and traits that are more regional. And while it is the case that you can't get to a regional trait by simply adding up local traits, there is no rigid barrier between the two types of traits (Corrington 2000b). Put differently, ordinal phenomenology describes traits wherever it finds them and can use both "empirical" and "ontological" data as part of its ongoing process of rendering nature and its orders intelligible.

Now we can begin our ordinal phenomenological description of the two cats who are not only on a mat. A thorough description must also include a temporal stretch in which the cats are observed doing a full variety of cat things, all pertinent to their identity as cats. Note that the temporality here is that of external

space-time transitions in nature, not the internal time-conscious-
ness of the transcendental ego (Husserl 1913) or of the future
driven temporality of the *Dasein* (Heidegger 1927a). Such intra-
self temporality is, of course, also part of the self-giving phenomenon for ordinal phenomenology but is not privileged over 'ontic',
natural time. In Husserl's tactic of bracketing existence claims,
the phenomenological reduction, he desired to put the so-called
"natural attitude" on hold while doing phenomenological work.
What he meant by the natural attitude has almost nothing to do
with aesthetic naturalism where the premium *is* placed on the
'natural' attitude. For Husserl what was meant was a kind of materialism combined with a one-dimensional scientism that operates with a highly reductive ontology and correlative blunt and
eliminative epistemology. This version of the natural attitude
would hamstring phenomenology from the start and severely limit
its sphere of operation to a fraction of the evident and self-showing.

Returning to our example, first, unlike the cat on the mat,
these cats have names, Plotinus and Darwin, that is, they have as
one of their traits, membership in a human partnership in which
naming confers an interspecies relationship guaranteeing caregiv-
ing over their lifetime. Their evolutionary success as a species has
been entwined with their co-membership in human communities.
Further, in having names, they are more likely to be the object of
anthropocentric projections from their caregivers.

One can do a standard description of the "ontic" physical appearance of the cats—black, medium-length hair, fifteen and
twelve pounds, two years old, etc. And one can describe their
personalities: Darwin is extraverted and a beggar whereas Plotinus is shy and never begs. These are traits that appear within the
standard phenomenal visual field and can be unfolded via standard transcendental phenomenology as it also lights up the acts of
consciousness by and through which the human transcendental

ego intends these traits. One can also phenomenologically intuit eating and sleeping habits, affection needs and patterns, play responses, fear triggers, and other modes of interaction with each other and the larger world. Even within the standard phenomenological model we have left the cat on the mat far behind.

When we shift to ordinal phenomenology proper we see how ordinal metaphysics provides phenomenology with the broadest horizon within which to work and we see how metaphysics in turn gets dressed out in the rich fabrics of nature in its fullest expression. As noted, all orders/natural complexes exist in innumerable orders and have innumerable subaltern orders. Many of these are ontic/empirical while others might be called ontological, although we need not depend on the latter term. Perhaps it is best to stick with the language of "greater or lesser scope."

We start the ordinal analysis on this broader level by noting that the cats belong to the order of siblings. They were littermates and have the same genetic heritage. They belong to the order of shelter cats who were rescued as opposed to the order of cats who were bred for show. They belong to the order of house cats because the condo association where they live forbids outdoor cats because of the havoc they cause to the bird population. They belong to the order of black cats and thus have the trait of being scary to certain superstitious people. They belong to the order of cats who only eat dry food. They belong to the order of cats who have not been raised with a dog. They now belong to the order of cats who have been used as a pedagogical devise in a book of philosophy. They belong to the order of animals that are referred to by me as "who" rather than as "that."

It must be stressed that each of these ordinal locations is just as real as the physical cat on the mat, only real in a different order and in a different respect. The dramatic shift to ontological parity opens up all of these locations and lets them have the full ontological presence that they deserve and demand. We can open up even further relational orders for the full whatness of the cats.

For example, the cats are both locations for the anti-rabies vaccine, that is, the vaccine has more scope, two more places to occupy, than before, so the cats are orders/complexes that extend the being of the vaccine. In describing the ordinal locations of the anti-rabies vaccine from its perspective, the cats would have to be included. Or consider the ontic fact that the cats are part of the economic well being of the veterinarian who treats them and that they are part of her family economy. Again, this trait is just as real, just as relevant to their catness as their black fur. It has been a standard prejudice of pre-ordinal metaphysics that it preferred highly selected and simply defined orders as paradigms for the 'really real.'

Or reflect on the fact that the two cats groom each other precisely where they can't reach themselves. This ontic fact is as much a part of a direct phenomenological description as any other. It has an evolutionary base that keeps it in the repertories of current cat behavior. There is no built-in limit to how far and how deep an ordinal phenomenological description can go once the gates have been opened by the commitment to ontological parity. We have come a very long way from Husserl's simple notion of bracketing and from the paradigm of seeing the sense data of a single unmoving cat on a single mat. Time and complexity have entered into the *what* of phenomenological intuiting.

We have had to let go of the traditional notion of seeing where the stress had been on a direct and immediate gaze at something spatially present in a triadic space-time phenomenal field. Yet, Husserl did argue for a rich domain of the *co-present* that also gives itself, at first, indirectly to phenomenological insight/intuition. The co-present can become present when the phenomenologist rotates the phenomenon around, in, and through a variety of 'takes' of it so as to locate it in appropriate orders each of which has order specific traits. In this sense classical phenomenology is already partly ordinal. The main thing that has held it back is it's privileging of the immediate visual field, that is, the sphere where there is the bindingness of the Evident. Ordinal phenomenology radicalizes both the notion of the Evident and the idea of the co-present.

Instead of speaking of the Evident, with its insistence on epistemic certainty, the ordinal approach accepts that there are an indefinite number of degrees and types of evidence facing phenomenological query into the more basic orders of nature. Further, there is also a suspicion of any perspective that tries to build a hierarchical scheme on the dubious foundation of some bare bones evident certainty. Ambiguity and trait shifting go all the way down although the latter may be exceedingly slow and pragmatically negligible from the standpoint of the working phenomenologist.

More significant is what ordinal phenomenology does to the idea of the co-given. Traditional examples of the muted presence of the co-present or co-given include a physical object like a cube. One can only see several aspects at once and yet make an intuition as to the missing aspects. Rotating the cube makes the co-present present. But this humble example only takes place on the same ontological plane, namely from physical geometric part to physical geometric part. From the ordinal perspective this is just the tip of the (ordinal) iceberg.

What happens when the co-given resides in a different ontological order from the given? Can we still refer to the introduced trait as truly co-given or are we imposing an ontological frame onto the free movement of phenomenology? Can we go from a physical given trait, say, to an abstract idea and claim that the latter is not only part of the same phenomenon but is also co-given? The ordinal scheme enables us to move into and out of orders of all kinds of constitution precisely because there is no one trait or genus that is held to be foundational for others. Put differently, there is no super trait into which everything else must be translated. Thus, any relevant trait is co-given in its own way and ordinal phenomenology, attuned to the opening power of ontological parity, can respond to each newly disclosed order roughly on that order's terms.

For example, Darwin and Plotinus are black furred meat eaters. These traits are physical and "ontic." Yet they are also, as noted, factors in their veterinarian's personal economy. This too is an ontic fact. But it isn't 'physical' in the same way that black fur is. Yet it is fully co-present. It is a symptom of conceptual laziness or lack of metaphysical creativity to cling to physical traits when they represent only one order among others, all equally real.

When we add possibilities to the picture we can see even more clearly how important ontological parity is to phenomenological description. Just as all actualities are equally real, so too are all possibilities. However, unlike many perspectives, especially process systems, ecstatic naturalism denies that there is a special *realm* of possibilities or that there exist something like *pure* possibilities (Buchler 1966; 1990: 129–185). Possibilities always occur within and among actualities. When certain actualities change, then certain relevant possibilities change. No reductive metaphysics can adequately deal with the ontology of possibilities, especially physicalisms, which have no place for non-physical possibilities.

Consider the possibility that one cat will die before the other. This has an almost 100 percent probability; just as does the statement that one cat will outlive the other. But this is not to say that the possibility of being predeceased is free floating in some astral world of pure unstained possibility. Often a deity, perhaps in a mental aspect, is envisioned as the eternal keeper of the realm of possibility. The ordinal framework rejects such a divine mind and insists that no possibility can prevail outside of a given set of actualities fully within nature.

Thus, Darwin has the possibility of never getting kidney disease and outliving Plotinus if Plotinus gets such a disease. In the latter case the possibility ceases to be a possibility and becomes an actuality, thereby changing its ordinal status. However, a course of treatment could reverse the damage done to the kidney so that the possibility of health could be re-actualized within that order. The point at issue is that possibilities can change and evolve within their pertinent order and that it is good metaphysics, and a good use of ontological parity, to say that possibilities are co-given or co-present to the ongoing intuitions of ordinal phenomenology.

We have seen here that the various principles of ordinality (order, complex, ordinal location, trait, subaltern trait, possibility/ actuality, and ontological parity) function in both metaphysics *and* phenomenology to expand and enrich the tools and insights that enable us to have a portrayal of nature of great breadth and depth. It is the contention of this essay that ordinal phenomenology is the most capacious method for understanding the complex *ways* in which nature gives itself to thought and experience. Aesthetic naturalism, as the ultimate metaphysical perspective animating this text, uses this radicalized form of phenomenology to coax out the hidden generic traits of the innumerable orders of the World; namely the domains of *nature natured*. Yet this phenomenological study also takes on the task of probing, and being probed by, the infinite unconscious of nature and the unconscious of the human process. This task calls for an ordinal psychoanalysis.

The ordinal reconstruction of psychoanalysis follows the same path as the ordinal reconstruction of phenomenology with the difference being that psychoanalysis is less a method and more of a medium through which the traits of the human process are understood in terms of the dialectic between consciousness and the unconscious. Key to *ordinal* psychoanalysis is its insistence that all analytic work, in both theory and practice, begins and ends with the vast infinite unconscious of nature from out of which the differently infinite unconscious of the human self emerges. Nature's unconscious is the depth dimension of and for all ideation and instinct, all archetypal expression, all of the gods and goddesses that enter into and then depart human history, and ultimately the phenomenon of the aesthetic sublime, which emerges as the crowning 'achievement' of nature's unconscious as its dialectic with human consciousness concresces into works of art and beauty.

Put differently, ordinal psychoanalysis moves beyond the hidden narcissism of classical Freudian drive theory, with its obsession with intra-individual erogenous fixations frozen in oral or anal expression, and relocates psychoanalysis in the much larger domain of the human/nature interaction of the selving process. Selving is the ongoing process of self-formation within the encompassing sweep of the innumerable orders of the human and extra-human orders of *nature natured*. If existential psychoanalysis quite rightly speaks of the given totality of the self as being-in-the-world, ordinal psychoanalysis, as a part of aesthetic naturalism, equally affirms that the selving process is fully embedded in a vast natural world not of its own making.

On the deepest level, the human process is stretched between the innumerable orders of *nature natured* and the unconscious potencies of *nature naturing*. Not only must the foundling self negotiate the oftimes treacherous waters of manifest nature and the orders of the world (worldhood), but it also must deal with the potencies that emerge from both its personal and collective unconscious, noting that the collective unconscious, that shared with all human beings, is itself rooted in the even deeper unconscious of nature. Thus we have four layers for ordinal psychoanalysis to deal with: (1) the orders of manifest nature otherwise termed "nature natured"; (2) the complexes of the personal unconscious; (3) the archetypal images and structures of the collective unconscious; and (4) the unruly ground of the unconscious of nature, otherwise termed "nature naturing."

A full ordinal psychoanalytic treatment of an emotional complex, for example, will require rotating it through the four adumbrated layers/levels just delineated. Suppose one has to deal with a stubborn mother complex in an analysand (patient). The first layer would require looking at the literal biological mother, if pertinent, to see how she impinges on the thwarted selving process. All aspects of her relation to the patient must be presented to the analyst. Next the personal unconscious has to be probed to see what autobiographical associations are activated by the mother's facticity. Here dream work, fantasy, (seemingly) random ideation, and perhaps a word association test, are used to flesh out the contour of the feeling-toned complex within the life-trajectory of the analysand. Next, although these are not strictly sequential stages as there is continual movement backward and forward, the maternal images have to be probed for their species-wide archetypal meaning, especially around the guiding archetype of the Great Mother, a powerful symbol of the whole Self. Dream work usually intensifies when this third layer is activated because it is a law of the selving process that the unconscious honors those who honor it by attending to its potencies and powers. Finally, the fourth layer begins to open when the potencies themselves become partially available for interaction with the selving process. It is on this level that the mysteries of *nature naturing* begin to reveal themselves in however dim a light.

As is the case in phenomenology, so too in psychoanalysis, the discipline of practicing ontological parity opens up many gates to the unconscious. Of course one can say, "the unconscious is as real as consciousness," but it is another to actually remain open and alert to the endless varieties of unconscious activities and contents. It is a simple "ontic" fact that consciousness has emerged from the unconscious of nature through an ancient and ongoing struggle that is never completely guaranteed or won. The human immersion in nature is total and unending and the enveloping sweep of the depth dimension of *nature naturing* often dwarfs the feeble powers of finite consciousness. For Jung, there is a moral layer to the consciousness/unconscious dialectic; namely, that it is a moral imperative to make as much material of the vast unconscious as conscious as possible, provided, in all cases, that the attending consciousness has the strength and resources to integrate and handle the alien, to it, material from 'below.' In other words, unconsciousness is a sin and is dangerous to boot.

This is not to say that all of the unconscious (personal, collective, and of nature) can be rendered conscious, but that those orders pertinent to the selving process must be as much as our finite powers and abilities allow. Perfection must be rejected as an ideal and wholeness must be sought instead. Consciousness has been strengthened by personal and social forms of semiosis, wherein sign systems have become habituated and secure the nascent self against the depths from which the sign systems have struggled free. The selving process has many resources at its disposal and can rely upon ancient human wisdom as well as upon current strategies of sign assimilation and manipulation to secure access to the multiple spheres of reality. Public semiotic codes can stabilize the self and protect its oftimes fragile consciousness against collapsing into a black hole of meaninglessness. At the same time, however, other public codes can impose their own kinds of closure and even the demonic onto the individual consciousness that seeks stability at all costs. For many, the prospect of an open semiotic universe is too anxiety provoking and they seek to reduce their existential freedom by grasping onto a very narrow range of rigid signs that guarantee an almost total reduc tion in anxiety but at a cost of reducing the amount of freedom that the individual or group can then have (Tillich 1952).

Ordinal psychoanalysis has the responsibility of studying all of the twists and turns of the selving process as it moves from the state of dreaming innocence in the literal and symbolic womb (*chora* as in Plato's *Timaeus*) to the fullness of life amidst the various potencies of *nature naturing*. Both "ontic" and "ontological" data will be part of the given and co-given for ordinal phenomenology and ordinal psychoanalysis, the former providing the method with the latter providing the medium, that is, psychoanalysis being the lens through which the phenomenal traits of the human process will be seen.

Put even more strongly, ordinal psychoanalysis will be the lens through which we will explore the fourfold of the individual selving process, the social and communal aspect of that very process, the religious dimension of the personal and social self, and then the culmination of the self, community, and religion, in the aesthetic sublime. This fourfold differs from that of Heidegger's four-ing of divinities, mortals, earth, and sky but rings together in much the same way, creating a world ring that is a binding vibration that gathers the four together into the Same. The metaphysical perspective animating the entire treatise is aesthetic naturalism, which roots all categories, all signs and sign systems, all modes and forms of selving, all social aggregates, all forms of religion, and all forms of transforming art in the perennial fissuring of the abyss between *nature naturing* and *nature natured*, always fundamentally different from each other, yet always the Same, the twin *ur*-vibrations of the one nature that there is, the two grounding tones perennially ringing within the fourfold—nature's ecstatic song ever ancient and ever new.

I

SELVING

The human process is the most infolded and multi-layered series of events and structures in the known orders of nature. It is fully a part of nature and derives its shifting contours from its sheer locatedness within the infinity of the uncountable complexes of *nature natured*. The human self is inexhaustible in its inner riches while yet being almost completely predictable in its behavior and idea formations. The products of the self-in-process are most often routinized and banal, but on the rare occasion they can open up the depths of nature and transform the lives of those fortunate enough to encounter and understand them. Randomness and sheer experiential drift mark the human process throughout most of its waking hours and the novel and creative are often denied instantiation in individual and social life. Simply put, we are often our own worst existential enemies, flattening out the multiple forms of semiosis that are available to us as members of a rich variety of sign-using communities.

The overall arc and trajectory of the human process, as embedded in the one nature that there, is herein termed "selving," to denote the built-in momentum that takes place from the barest origins of the fragile and nascent self through the externalizations of semiotic life, to the return of the lost object of the pre-self stage as concresced in the life and symbols of religion and art. Selving is a strong force and power within nature and has its 'home' within the human process. It, like anything else 'alive,' is subject to multiple forms of pathology, some of which will be treated here. Yet selving also has an uncanny inner power to heal the attendant self and reweave the torn fabric of its life. If Jung speaks of the archetype of the Self as the *imago Dei* within, aesthetic naturalism prefers to speak of the potencies of *nature naturing* and, ultimately of the Will in the sense of Schopenhauer. And within the pulsating heart of the Will to life is the deeper stillness of what Plotinus called the One. Note that Schopenhauer is not speaking of the Will to *live* but of the Will to *life* (*Wille zum Leben*), where the latter term connotes a sense of fecundity that perennially springs forth with unending potency.

Most important is the primal fact that the selving process is shriven by the natural difference between *nature naturing* and *nature natured*. To be shriven is to be opened up and shaken by the natural difference. *Nature naturing* is encountered as the unconscious of nature and represents the uncanny, the powerful, the alien, the abject, yet also the meaningful, and the purposive, albeit within certain limits. On the other side of the fissuring of nature, the innumerable orders of 'available' nature, that is, *nature natured*, the self is awash with an endless ocean of public signs and sign systems—an actual infinite of semiosis with neither beginning nor culmination. We are semiotic through and through, as are animals and plants within the spheres studied by zoosemiotics and biosemiotics. Animals in particular live in species-specific *Umwelten*, but do not inhabit self-conscious life-worlds as we do. In other words, animals can read signs but they do not know that they *are* signs. Certain primates might be an exception to this. In our case we inhabit both ancient *Umwelten* (environments) *and* life-worlds and there is often a conflict between an *Umwelt* that was once a valuable adaptation in our evolutionary past but is now, under different environmental conditions, an actual maladaptation—that split being known as an evolutionary "time lag." Hence the human process is a mixture of working and no longer working adaptations.

Probing into the fissuring between *nature naturing* and *nature natured* takes care and patience, with abjection always a factor even for an ordinal phenomenological account. In addition, ordinal psychoanalysis must itself use care in deploying the right categories in the right way if we are to see the selving process *in situ*. The tools at our disposal are powerful but the forces of abjection and denial are also powerful. The commitment to ontological parity will continue to be one of the most potent tools we have in getting past abjection and denial.

The human process, then, is a highly complex and multi-layered phenomenon within nature that is uniquely open to both sides of the natural difference. It is the one order within nature-as-known that can probe into the natural difference and can transform itself through this very process of probing into the difference. All of the categories of semiotics, the systematic study of those orders in nature known as signs and sign systems, come home to roost in the selving process, precisely because selving probes deeply down into the womb of the unconscious of nature from whence proto-signs come on their way to becoming positioned signs within nature and human communities.

What we can also call "psychosemiosis" seeks a unified theory of the basic structures and behaviors of those signs that are relevant, directly or indirectly, to the human process. Ordinal psychoanalysis is that branch of psychosemiotics that focuses most directly on the pathology and healthy aspects of selving per se. Whereas psychosemiotics, for example, might have a theory of perception, say, in Peirce's concept of the correlation of the percept and perceptual judgment within the percipuum, or an analysis of the thought processes in reasoning with signs, as in Dewey's analysis of pragmatic reasoning, ordinal psychoanalysis is concerned with the struggle between health and pathology in the quest for finite meaning within the selving process.

The task ahead is thus to phenomenologically describe the selving process from its beginnings in the birthing event to its trajectory through the individuation process of adolescence, to adulthood, and through its numerous ramifications and correlations with semiosis both public and private. Communal, religious, and aesthetic dimensions pertinent to selving will receive more detailed treatment in the subsequent chapters.

Ordinal phenomenology works with both *categories* in the standard sense, like separation, return, or transformation, and *metaphors* like, dreaming innocence, the material maternal, and the domain of the father, on the other. Care and precision are called for. In recent philosophy, and above all in theology, metaphorical construction and deconstruction has favored metaphor over the use of categories in, say, Aristotle's sense. The shift to metaphorics need not entail an anti-realism since metaphors too have to work, have to function with their neighbors in a complex symphony of notes that all work toward a coherent and knowable vision of the orders of the world. The ideal is to have a robust use of categories working in a rich and multi-layered series of dialectical engagements with very carefully chosen metaphors. There is no need, and dubious value, in choosing categories over metaphors, or vice versa, or in arguing that one is more liberating and the other more confining, or that the use of categories must produce a static ontology while metaphorics leads only to a narcissistic display of rootless *jouissance*. Philosophy advances when both metaphor and category render some regnant aspect of nature available to public scrutiny and appraisal. And it is only jointly that metaphors and categories can produce a metaphysics worthy of its true birthright.

With that proviso we move directly into the initial momentum
of the selving process in the dim and dark domain of the pre-self
in the literal maternal womb which is itself the gateway to the
womb of *nature naturing* in one direction and the opening out
into *nature natured* in the other. The selving process derives its
often fierce momentum from the deep underground potencies of
nature's unconscious that surround it in the biological womb. For
Plato the *chora*/womb is the open receptacle within which, and by
means of which, the orders of form and matter are brought together by the deity who is an artist-of-being rather than some *Demi-
urge*
kind of creator in a monotheistic sense. This finite god can only
do what he does because the *chora* makes all unifying action
possible. The *chora* brings the two extremes of reality together;
namely, the eternal and unchanging realm of the forms and the
changing traitless sheer becoming of the realm of matter. The
cosmic womb enables the finite god to wed time and eternity, to
create the orderly universe and put each formed thing in its proper place within a closed cosmos. The universe itself is eternal and
had no state of pre-existence nor will it have a state of post-
existence, just an endless reiteration of cyclic forms. *First principle.*

The analogical bridge from Plato's *chora*/receptacle to the human womb is direct. The chora is the space of spaces that enables
physical space to house all that is spatially configured by the relevant forms/archetypes. The fetus is provided with its matter and
form by its maternal receptacle and enters into its morphogenesis
along ancient patterns and pathways that make its very being at all
possible. In a sense, the human womb is even more potent than
Plato's *chora* in that it also is 'responsible' for giving the fetus
some of its own material substance and its own archetypal material, with the augmentation provide by the male sperm. The fetus is
a moment of becoming for the womb itself as well as an autonomous order in its own right. Individuation starts with cell division

and continues throughout the earthly life cycle of the individual
and perhaps beyond mortal existence.

The energy that goes into fetal development is rooted in the
depth dimension of nature, ultimately in the pulsations of *nature
naturing*. Earlier Schopenhauer's fundamental concept of the
Will was invoked as an equivalent to *nature naturing*, and is especially useful when dealing with the human process in its mode of
selving. As in aesthetic naturalism Schopenhauer divides nature
into two dimensions that stand in intimate relation to each other
even though they are ontologically utterly distinct. His parallel to
nature naturing and *nature natured* is the World as Will and the
World as Representation, or Presentation (*Vorstellung*).

The Will is a unified momentum 'underneath' the phenomenal
world that we experience through the senses and the categories of
the Kantian mind. Will is without form or goals, it has neither
telos nor a meaningful history, and it plays no favorites in nature.
It pushes its way into and through all things, especially in the
organic orders. It is a Will to Life, to intense manifestation and
expression. It produces conflict between and among the orders of
nature as not all can thrive at the same time at the same space.
Life is overly abundant and competition is ubiquitous. The Will
produces nature by objectifying itself into infinite centers of willing that are thereby governed by the triad of space, time, and
causality. The Will (*nature naturing*) is profligate and unrelenting
in its eternal othering into the orders we know as *nature natured*.
And, most importantly, we know it directly when we look within
ourselves and feel it operating in our own bodies. Epistemologically, the Will is closer to us than the manifest orders of nature,
which are the objectification of the Will. In essence, I feel the
Will coursing through my body—an expression of what Peirce
would call secondness; namely, brute impaction from something
that is uniquely both inside and outside the self, and by extrapola-
tion I feel this Will operating in all things:

Not only in those phenomena that are quite like his own, in
human beings and animals, will he acknowledge the same will
as their innermost essence, but further reflection will lead him
to recognize as well the force that drives and vegetates in
plants, even the force by which crystals form, that turns the
magnet toward the North Pole, that produces a shock when
two heterogeneous metals are brought into contact. . . . It is
that which is innermost, the core of every individual thing and
likewise of the whole: it makes its appearance in every blindly
effectual natural force; it also makes its appearance in the re-
flectively considered actions of human beings. (Schopenhauer
1819: 148)

So, while we have our initial contact to the will through an
awakening to our bodily sensations, we quickly, through a natural
kind of empathy, experience the same Will coursing through other human beings, and then, from there we sense the will in animals, then plants, and then, finally, in inorganic orders. Ultimately we experience the Will to Life within the entire cosmos but
with special intensity within the human order where the will also
produces the most suffering. Here Schopenhauer argues that
high intelligence causes greater suffering because it can imagine
sufferings that go beyond actual sufferings thus stoking the flames
of 'real' suffering. On the curve of mentality and suffering, the
genius suffers the most, as we shall see in chapter 4.

Aesthetic naturalism affirms Schopenhauer's brilliant analysis
of the Will but rejects his Kantian epistemology and phenomenal-
ism. The current perspective can also be called a naturalistic
pragmatic realism that locates mind as an evolutionary product of
nature, not as the Kantian shaper of a chaotic manifold molded *a
priori* according to eternal principles of pure and practical reason.
A priori structures do exist but they are understood to be pragmatic in origin and subject to sequent testing as abductions and
transcendental arguments. The objectivized orders of nature (*nature natured*) are no more a human contrivance than the Grand

Canyon is a social construction. Of course, the categorical and existential analysis of 'objective' nature can take on an endless variety of forms but nature still gets a veto when pragmatic methods are used in a careful and thorough way. There is a link between pragmatism and ordinal phenomenology insofar as both are driven to find ways of letting nature's own voices speak underneath (or above) the choruses of the human-all-too-human.

The Will pours itself into the fetus as it takes on the momentum of its inner/outer morphogenesis. It stakes its claim, makes its mark, takes what it needs, and concretizes the Will in its own trajectory toward post-natal existence. It issues its demands, develops its archetypal forms and its partial uniqueness in certain of its traits always furthering the pulsations of the Will to Life, which drives its whole nascent being. The maternal womb shelters and protects it, provides all of its nutrition, and empowers its budding selving process. The biological mother reenacts the ancient drama of the dance of the Will as it surges through her maternal body providing the power and reserve energy needed to transform what starts as simple cell division into creating the most complex organism in the currently known universe.

When the fetus becomes a viable being outside of the womb it starts its pilgrimage within the indefinite orders of nature that at first seem to have no sharp contour or even basic structure. The senses need to develop and the organism needs to adjust to a vastly different post-womb world where the structures and forces of space, time, and causality take on astonishing layers and folds of complexity compared to the enclosed world of the preceding months. Resistance (secondness) carves out an inner and outer trajectory that marks the beginning of the selving process as the nascent self activates its drive mechanisms and opens out its erogenous zones. The Will continues to push the life energies outward into an endless stream of encounters between the fledgling self and the seemingly opaque world just beyond the maternal body and breast.

The world of dreaming innocence (Tillich) is violently left behind as the not-yet-self experiences an ontological break between the fluidity of the womb world and the decidedly less fluid and noise and light filled world of external *nature natured*. The contours of the world emerge along with, and because of, the earliest momenta of selving in the infant. We must use the "because of" with care here as the infant's selving process is not a simple unfolding from a purely internal entelechy but is a complex evolutionary mechanism that involves external triggers before the inner process can *un*fold. These triggers work on pre-given archetypal material that has been fine-tuned for millions of years thus assuring basic evolutionary competence for all cases where a negative mutation is not found. Looked at from the opposite direction, there would be no triggers if the archetypes weren't already in place to be fired as needed and necessary by the emerging organism.

The parallelism between trigger and firing of the archetype is tight and a closed system. There is little room for the free play of either the efficient causal trigger or the archetypal emergent effect on the most basic level of transaction. The momenta of the Will are strong and highly directed and any discussion of free will will have to be postponed until later in our analysis.

Before looking into the outward momenta of the nascent self of the oral, anal, and genital stages, stages and drive zones that we will deconstruct from the standpoint of self-psychology (Kohut), we must probe into the unconscious origins of the selving process that are antecedent to the physical birth itself but which surround, sustain, and oftimes haunt or realign the self in its unfolding and re-infolding. This pre-birth self has been glimpsed through a glass darkly by Kant in his analysis of the roots of transcendental subjectivity in the schematism and the transcendental unity of apperception as shaped and lit-up by time—in Heidegger's reading of the daring move Kant makes in the first edition of the First Critique. But the most detailed and complete analysis of the pre-conscious root of the selving process is found in Schopenhauer's analysis of the layers of subjectivity as they shape the ethical character of the individual. Schopenhauer distinguishes between the intelligible, empirical, and acquired characters, with the intelligible (*noumenal*) being the most important for our portrayal of the pre-conditions of the selving process.

The intelligible character is our ultimate character, which is eternal and relatively unchanging and which is only partly known by us as we unfold its nature throughout our empirical lives. It is who we are in our deepest unconscious depths, prior to the unfolding of the self under the conditions of space, time, and causality. The intelligible character cannot be changed by our more well known acquired and empirical characters as these too are shaped by the imperial power of the intelligible character. Schopenhauer pushes for a rather hard determinism concerning human character. But he leaves a very important door open at the other end of the human journey that can quicken the selving process and move it toward a genuine overcoming of the constraints of the intelligible character. He does this through the power of art and, differently, through the deliverance found in both Advaita Vedanta Hinduism and in Buddhism's denial of the Will.

The pre-temporal, pre-spatial, and pre-causal intelligible character is individuated, that is, it is unique to each individual and stays with each person through his or her various reincarnations. From this perspective the intelligible character is karma; namely, the locus of the moral law that envelopes and controls each monadic self on its pilgrimage through innumerable human personalities and egos. It can be changed but only when the attending ego grasps its basic contour in direct personal terms and realizes that only strenuous moral energy can modify its karmic directionality and structure. Much of this work is done between incarnations, while much remains to be done in incarnate states, especially through the direction of philosophy. For Schopenhauer, liberation from a negative intelligible character is available through the philosophical appreciation of aesthetic works of genius, especially music, and the Buddhistic denial of the all-consuming Will to Life.

Schopenhauer argues that the intelligible character, as discovered by Kant, is the transcendental condition for the observable and highly conditioned empirical character and the learned acquired character:

> The intelligible character of any person is to be regarded as an extra-temporal, thus indivisible and unalterable, act of will, of which the empirical character is the phenomenon, developed and elaborated within space and time and all the forms belonging to the Principle of Sufficient Ground, as that character is experientially displayed in the person's entire manner of action and course of life. (Schopenhauer 1819: 342)

The Principle of Sufficient Ground asserts that there is a reason for everything that happens within the orders of *nature natured*, hence the determining grounds of the empirical character are set in the phenomenal realm but as rooted in the noumenal. Schopenhauer has a double-barreled determinism; first, the intelligible character is determined by an act of will that is outside of the world of space, time, and causality, and second, the intelligible character determines the empirical character as it operates in the phenomenal realm.

The fetus is surrounded with its own individuated intelligible character, its karmic heritage that is at least as ancient as the human species itself. It has remained mostly the same throughout a series of dimly lit incarnations where it has shaped and patterned behavior and ideation along highly inertial pathways. For the emergent fetus, the karmic envelope is its ultimate enabling condition as it provides the *how* and *what* of its unconscious psyche and also serves as its direct link to the unconscious of nature. The intelligible character, the noumenal depths of the self-in-process, is stretched across eternity yet participates in temporality through its effects on the empirical (ontic) self. The empirical self is the known personality of the individual; namely, the self as seen and grasped by others and by simple or complex introspection. My empirical character falls into patterns that are predicable and quantifiable by routinized testing procedures. When the empirical character is well known and understood, one can make predictions about future behavior and ideations, making its lack of freedom akin to that of the intelligible character. A careful study of one's empirical character can thus shed light on its parallels with the depth dimension of the intelligible character. Both are largely determined and resist transformation by normal means.

Can one talk about a pre-birth intelligible character outside of the concept of reincarnation? For Kant it is possible to posit this transcendental unity that is the formal *I-think* that grounds and founds the *a posteriori* aspects of the self. In his ethical theory his analysis of the good will, the only thing in the universe that is good per se, he has a structure that is a noumenal foundation for the empirical moral being that does not entail reincarnation. It is a given, if somewhat astonishing, fact at the basis of our ethical existence. And I think that one can take on Schopenhauer's model of the intelligible character in a similar Kantian way; namely, that it is a built-in transcendental structure that appears *a priori* in the nascent self. In good Kantian fashion we cannot ask about its whence and whither as it is a noumenon beyond experience but we can posit it as a hidden transcendental condition for the possibility of the empirical self known within finite human experience as shaped by space, time, and causality. Aesthetic naturalism, as a metaphysical perspective, does not logically entail a belief in reincarnation, but it does remain largely friendly to the idea for a variety of reasons that will emerge as the analyses and phenomenological descriptions unfold further.

The depth dimension of the nascent self is rooted in the unconscious of nature, the dark and taciturn momenta of *nature naturing*. For Heidegger the fundamental difference is the "ontological difference" between being and any thing-in-being, whereas for ecstatic naturalism it is the "natural difference" between *nature naturing* and *nature natured* that bisects the self-in-process. This difference is the fundamental fissure that opens out within the self, differentiating the unconscious from the conscious. The power of the unconscious is great and much of human evolution has been devoted to ways to lessen its imperial power over the weak powers of consciousness and individuation. The phylogenetic struggles against nature's unconscious are recapitulated ontogenetically within each selving process.

It might be too romantic to argue that nature propels humans into higher consciousness in order to get a glimpse of itself through human consciousness, but there does seem to be a drive within our species in particular for intense individuation, for a movement away from the dark background of unconsciousness and toward a self-awareness that only human consciousness can bring. This idea requires a kind of meta-teleology that takes us far beyond the prospects of an ordinal phenomenology, where teleological ideas are probed as they operate within the human process in very limited, and usually frustrated, ways. We must use more circumspect language when describing the travails of fitful and finite consciousness as it sheds more and more light on its own origin in nature's unconscious depths.

The self, then, is opened to its depths by the internal fissuring of the natural difference between *nature naturing*, nature's unconscious, and *nature natured*, the innumerable orders of the world. Yet from the very beginning the nascent self abjects its own unconscious as well as its deeper roots in the unconscious in nature and this is as must be for individuation and consciousness to emerge at all. The very realization of the natural difference may never come at all as the selving process gets stalled at a primitive level where the surging potencies of the unconscious are projected outward and not allowed to become actual to the attending self. For Jung, such oblivion to one's own unconscious, personal and collective, is an analogue to sin; namely, it is, or can be, a dangerous ignorance that makes the self vulnerable to undigested raw powers that can eclipse the nascent and emergent 'autonomous' self. It is a 'sin' in the sense that it represents a disobedience to the demands for growth and wisdom that the selving process calls for from the self-in-process.

This represents a careful balancing act. On the one hand, the unconscious, personal, collective, and that of nature, needs to be abjected long enough for consciousness to emerge and define its own autonomous territory, to push outward into the orders of *nature natured* and negotiate its needs and desires with other individuating selves. The selving process cannot get off the ground if the unconscious is not split off in a dramatic abjection that pushes it even further away from the conscious ego. Consciousness arises into its fragile sphere where its independence is prey to sudden reversals in which it is flooded with unconscious contents and energies. For ancient humans this flooding was more common than it is for us and religious rituals were developed in an effort to gain some control over the process of the seeming loss of self. Yet for us the danger may be even greater as the energy going into abjecting may be intensified with the greater power of consciousness and its needs for total autonomy. But, as argued by Tillich, autonomy is a fragile structure held in place by a social harmony that relies on a free sphere of rational interaction among members of a community holding enlightenment values in common. Such an 'ideal' social system is especially vulnerable because autonomy is not strong enough to be self-grounding and is always vulnerable to forces coming from the depths of the unconscious that can shatter the world of autonomy.

This is not to assert that the unconscious is simply demonic or anti-reason but that it will act as if it is if it is not integrated into the life of consciousness at all points of the individuation process. Integration of the potencies of nature and the archetypes of the collective unconscious, along with the complexes of the personal unconscious are all required if the selving process is to be fulfilled and the relations between the conscious ego and its depths is to be brought to a meaning-filled consummation under the conditions of finitude.

An awareness of the natural difference, in whatever language or terminology, is crucial for the successful navigating of the selving process. From the eternity-in-time of the intelligible character, through the oral, anal, and genital drives (to be deconstructed), to the emergence of the actual self that can mirror itself in a growing list of others, we see a variety of attempts to both find and lose the depth dimension of *nature naturing*. The key feature is that consciousness needs to become strong enough to arc back from its multi-form interactions within the innumerable orders of *nature natured* to enter into and to withstand the pulsations of *nature naturing* that give it the potencies it needs to have a fuller and more powerful existence under the conditions of finitude.

We have seen how the intelligible character molds the empirical character. The intelligible character is known by an abduction that goes from the study of the empirical character through a rule, the abduction proper, which then explains the nature of what causes the empirical character to be what it is. The reincarnation theory makes it easier to explain how the intelligible character correlates to the ontic/empirical individual, although one could argue that it just pushes the argument back in time and still has to deal with the first time a soul emerged from the pre-human or animal group soul to the human soul—an evolutionary question of human origins.

The reincarnation theory that the current perspective endorses is that all living things have some kind of soul, however primitive. Plants and animals have group souls that are not individuated. In some animal species there are hints of individuation, say, for example, in domesticated dogs. These tiny moments of individuation get passed on to the group soul edging it ever so slowly toward distinctness and potential individuation. Humans belong to their own species-specific group soul as well; however, they also have an individuated and at least partly unique personal soul with its own subjective contents and memories. At the death of the physical body subjective self-consciousness continues in a different kind of embodiment. Process theology rejects this notion of subjective immortality for a form of objective immortality in which only the memories and contents of the self continue as remembered by the consequent nature of god (Hartshorne 1984). The self for whom these were memories is extinguished at death. In this sense, process theology is closer to Buddhism while ecstatic naturalism is somewhat closer to Advaita Vedanta Hinduism with its notion of Atman as reincarnating in a hidden continuity behind the innumerable empirical egos that are born and die with each incarnation. The self that reincarnates is a mixture of the given finite personality and the eternal Atman that is identical with Brahman, the ultimate.

As Platonic myth has it, the freshly incarnating self crosses the river of forgetfulness taking a drink from its dark waters before incarnating in yet another human body. Consequently, the new ego has only the dimmest memory, if that, of its previous lives as it slowly embeds itself in its new densely physical life-form. Nature casts a veil of ignorance around the soul so that it can concentrate on its new incarnation free from the burdens and joys of its previous life/lives. Nature, ever the pragmatist, cuts off the flow of information because it would quickly overwhelm the self with its sheer almost infinite magnitude—perhaps encompassing hundreds of thousands of incarnations just in the human or proto-human orders. The self may initiate its spiritual journey whether it believes in reincarnation or not. In either case the logic of individuation is the same; namely, to slowly and carefully nego-tiate the emergence of the selving process in an ongoing dialectic between the modes of the unconscious and the strengthening powers of consciousness.

We now return from these points of pre-conscious origin and their relation to the rise of consciousness to the more specific domains of the emergence of the proto-self in infancy and its locus for the drives as analyzed by classical Freudian metapsy-chology. The drive theory assumes that the human being func-tions in a way that is directly analogous to mechanical and fluid dynamics in the physical orders of nature. The basic model, as further developed by Wilhelm Reich, is that of build-up and re-lease, where a flow of energy, in this case sexual, moves along a channel and meets resistance from a repressing force which pushes that energy back against itself so that it cannot be ex-pressed in the way it was meant to be. This causes the sexual or aggressive energy to root around to find another place to express itself, this other place being a sublimated outlet that is only indi-rectly sexual and hence 'safe' for the organism.

The infant's primitive ontology starts with the breast from which its nourishment and sheer power of being comes. It is the point of origin that remains in the background throughout the lifetime of the individual but gets translated into an endless varie-ty of self-objects; namely, objects that have an uncanny ability to be present in the simple and obvious sense as items within the domains of *nature natured*, yet also having hidden roots in the unconscious of nature. The term "transitional object" only cap-

tures part of the dynamics of these substitute objects. For Kristeva, the "good breast" haunts the self-in-process as the infant navi-
gates the world of signs and language, eventually substituting language for the lost breast of mother identity.

The so-called oral phase exists before the subject-object di-
chotomy emerges fully for the infant. It is a continuation of the
dreaming innocence of the womb although it begins the manifestation of the birth trauma that will also haunt the self throughout
its trajectory in time. It is important to note that the birth trauma
is as much an ontological as a personal event. In the realm of
dreaming innocence there is no split between *nature naturing*
and *nature natured,* as there is no split between self and other.
For Freud only the oceanic fluidity exists for the fetus, and the
emergent self longs for that oceanic bliss for the rest of its life,
substituting one attraction after another to recapture that feeling
prior to its expulsion from the garden of earthly delights.

The birth trauma emerges from the fact of the natural difference that propels the self outward into the endless involvements
of the innumerable orders of *nature natured.* It begins to feel its
littleness, its finitude, its sheer locatedness as but one lonely order within a vast nature that does not exist for its own benefit.
Pathology can easily emerge here as these stark realizations may
prove too hard for the nascent ego to take in and a form of
psychic inflation may compensate by producing fantasies of power and delusions of grandeur. For Otto Rank this "primal trauma"
lies at the foundation of individual existence and of civilization:

> We have thus surveyed the whole circle of human creation,
> from the nocturnal wish-dream to the adjustment to reality, as
> an attempt to materialize the primal situation—i.e., to undo
> the primal trauma. From this survey the so-called advance in
> the development of civilization has proved to be a continually
> repeated attempt to adjust to the enforced removal from the
> mother the instinctive tendency to return to her. . . . In the
> course of our arguments we have evaded the question as to

how it comes about that the striving for the recovery of the
pleasurable primal situation in the womb, recognized as the
primary tendency of the libido and regarded by us as an expression of the greatest possibility of pleasure, is bound up in
so inseparable a way with primal anxiety. . . . This experienced
anxiety is thus the first content of perception, the first psychic
act, so to say, to set up barriers; and in these we must recognize the primal repression against the already powerful tendency to re-establish the pleasurable situation just left. (Rank
1924: 103, 186–187)

This struggle with abjection produces a momentum that gener-
ates anxiety for the nascent self as it makes its first moves away
from the oceanic bliss of the womb. I have been arguing that the
birth trauma is as much an "ontic" event as an "ontological" transition. As ontic it is a violent phase transition from fluidity to the
harsh demands of solid tri-dimensionality, while as ontological it
is the ejection from *nature naturing* to *nature natured*. The birth
trauma, as passionately described by Rank, is the primal advent of
the selving process and is re-enacted in myriad ways throughout
existence under the sway of space, time, and causality. Anxiety
sets up barriers or armoring rings against the return to the primal
origin and this produces neurosis. Both Rank and Reich see anxiety as a product of internal psychic conflict resulting from
blocked energy flows, whether back to the symbolic womb or out
of the orgone ocean that envelopes the self. While Rank came to
distance himself a little from his early theory of the birth trauma it
remains an important addition to the categorical resources of
psychoanalysis and helps explain the sheer energy invested in the
longing for conditions of origin.

In the oral phase, then, the infant lives in the connection with
the maternal and derives pleasure form sucking on the maternal
breast. But the drives of the psyche continue to push from within
and the infant shifts his or her focus to an anal fixation where the
anus becomes the next erogenous zone. This shift represents,

according to classical theory, a movement away from direct maternal fixation toward a nascent sense of the self as in some sense discontinuous from the breast and the mother. The next step for drive theory is the all-important genital stage where sexual awakening unfolds from and through the highest and most mature erogenous zone. Oral and anal fixations still exist and can still exert their peculiar lure in sexual pathologies and fetishes but the genital awakening represents the promise of healthy sexuality.

For Wilhelm Reich, full genital potency emerges when biological/sexual energy flows free from the muscular and characterological armoring that had held it back from fully expressing itself. Reich translates Freud's theories into a more literal energetics of sexual currents that flow through all living things and which are even found in the non-living orders of nature. His theory of "orgone" was meant to augment the classical theory of electro-magnetism by adding a layer of energy that is subtler and more primordial than the energies dealt with by physics. Orgone is the inner energy of all things but especially of the human being and has its highest manifestation in human sexuality. For Reich:

> In the atmosphere, in the soil, and in the living organism there exists a type of energy which acts in a specifically biologically way and which I have called "orgone." With the aid of the orgonoscope, this energy is visible as scintillation in the atmosphere and in the soil as well as on bushes (in the summer). . . . The specific biological energy does not exist "on the other side"; it is not metaphysical. It exists physically in the atmosphere and is demonstrable visually, thermically, and electroscopically. . . . For the time being, it must be assumed that orgone is the medium in which the electromagnetic waves of light vibrate. (Reich 1940; cited in Corrington 2003g: 190, 200–201)

For Reich then, orgone energy permeates the universe and is more basic than electromagnetism. It is elusive and functions in a wave-like way moving in vast cosmic currents that surround and penetrate the human organism. Orgone energy is benign and reaches its highest expression in the known universe in the human orgasm. The core of the self is unarmored and positive orgone energy that 'wishes' to move outward into orgonotic expression with another self through sexual entwinement. But armoring rings prevent orgone energy from a normal expression of itself thus producing the myriad forms of psychopathology that haunt the selving process.

Reich started out as a fairly classical Freudian but quickly moved in the direction of a more literal physical understanding of psychic phenomena as themselves involving orgonotic vibrations and waves that permeate the universe and that were present at cosmogenesis. He envisioned the body as being constituted by a series of armored zones that hold orgone/sexual energy in check so that its normal flowing outward into sexual expression is thwarted and dammed up thereby producing neurotic symptoms. As the armoring increases so does the co-occurant anxiety—a product of undischarged orgone energy. Thus there is a basic dialectic between sexual release and orgasmic potency on the one hand and the acute anxiety that comes from the damming of sexual energy on the other hand. His system rests on a simple energetic model:

> The simultaneous identity and antithesis of living and nonliving matter is most easily demonstrated in the orgone-biophysical formula of living functioning. It is the basic formula of biological pulsation: MECHANICAL TENSION → ENERGY CHARGE → ENERGY DISCHARGE → MECHANICAL RELAXATION. It applies to the pulsation of the heart as well as to the motion of the worm or the contraction of the vorticella. (Reich 1940; cited in Corrington 2003g: 196)

If there is too much mechanical tension in the organism anxiety increases as the organism seeks a way of releasing that high quantity. In those who are genitally potent, an energy discharge takes place that produces the stasis of relaxation. It's as simple as that. But such a state is rare among humans as armoring rings block healthy channels of discharge and keep back healthy orgonotic functioning.

Note that Reich's idea of orgastic potency is a subtle one. It requires a total alignment of the self with nature and the healthy world of intersubjectivity. Promiscuity, for Reich, was a sign of a deep pathology, that is, of a failure to attain a connection with the orgone ocean of the universe, requiring an addictive and compulsive acting out of genital sexuality with little genuine potency and no sense of attaining the true "pleasure premium."

For Reich, fixation on the oral and anal stages represents the result of armoring in which the self can only experience pleasure in a tightly circumscribed way. He distanced himself from the idea that psychoanalysis needed to open out specific memories of sexual traumas from childhood and thereby affect a catharsis that would enable the individual to open out a deeper relationship to sexual energy in a genital relationship. His materialism was of a strong and striking variety. What the psychoanalyst needed to do was not to invoke memory images that in turn would unblock the psyche, but to go deeper down into the musculature where the psychic armoring has its roots. It must be remembered that for Reich, repression and denial happen in the body, the muscles in particular, not just in the mind per se, and that no release from their power can be had that doesn't also work directly on the body itself. Once the knot in the armored musculature is released a great rush of emotion follows, as the orgone flow is set free for direct expression.

Reich, unlike Freud, believed that the basic human drives were positive in nature and that Freud remained stuck on the secondary drives like aggression and sexual pathology, thereby failing to see the positive core drive of orgone energy that was life-enhancing in all respects. It is no exaggeration to say that Reich was the most optimistic of the early psychoanalysts concerning not only the true nature of the human psyche/soma but also concerning the rate and possibilities of cure that orgonotic psychoanalysis could produce. In fact, Reich stopped referring to himself as a psychoanalyst as his orgone biophysics developed a more cosmic dimension.

What is of value in Reich's theories for the current perspective is his placement of the drive theory of Freud's metapsychology into a broader energetics that went beyond the limited perspective of the infantile erogenous zones. This ties in well with Kohut's own rejection of drive theory and its fixation on the very limited role that these zones actually play in autogenesis. For Kohut, the nascent self is only tied into an erogenous zone if its own narcissism fails to develop due to a failure of one or both parents to function as a stable self-object for the nascent self. The loss of self makes the individual vulnerable to a counter pull by the oral or anal erogenous zone because at least there is a modicum of pleasure to be had and, through that, some minimal sense of identity and continuity. For Kohut:

> It is the self of the child that, in consequence of the severely disturbed empathic responses of the parents, has not been securely established, and it is the enfeebled and fragmentation-prone self that (in the attempt to reassure itself that it is alive, even that it exists at all) turns defensively toward pleasure aims through the stimulation of erogenic zones, and then, secondarily, brings about the oral (and anal) drive orientation and the ego's enslavement to the drive aims correlated to the stimulated body zones. . . . If the self is seriously damaged, however, or destroyed, then the drives become powerful constellations in their own right. In order to escape from depression, the child turns from the unempathic or absent self-object to oral, anal, and phallic sensations, which he experiences with great intensity. (Kohut 1977: 74, 122)

Kohut brilliantly outflanks Freud's drive theory by arguing that the drives are not basic to the infant but only emerge when the infant has not succeeded in creating a minimal sense of self because the parents did not provide a venue for it to develop a healthy narcissism and its concurrent self-image. Without proper mirroring from the mother and an idealization through the father, the infant cannot find a stable sense of itself as an integral self-in-the-making. The infant senses that it may fragment and lose its sense of being a totality over and against the world. The resultant depression represents a withdrawal of psychic energy to the unconscious as it has no role to play in building up the nascent self-image. The infant then reacts to this energy withdrawal by grasping at the erogenous zones where the energy can return from the unconscious and reignite a sense of aliveness. This vividness is, of course, a compromise formation and in the end holds the self back from becoming an integral adult. Freud's big mistake was to confuse a pathogenic state with a normal process of development. For Kohut, the narcissistically healthy infant and child simply don't need to become fixated on the erogenous zones. Thus for both Reich and Kohut the Freudian obsession with the infantile erogenous zones shows a serious lack of insight into how, even in infancy, a larger sense of self emerges that cannot be reduced to part-self zones of stimulation.

What the nascent self needs is its own special ontology that moves it into its post dreaming innocence phase. It needs to emerge more fully from the unconscious, or pre-conscious, and to find its spatial, temporal, and causal correlations within its expanding sense of the uncountable orders of *nature natured*. Each sense needs to be correlated to its proper object and relational sphere and it needs to work in consort with the other senses so that the environment activates the species-specific *Umwelt* of the human process. The *Umwelt* precedes the Life World in time and remains the bedrock of our evolutionary heritage. It functions regardless of the travails of the Life World or the Horizon of the self-in-process. The concept of "Horizon" has more scope than that of "Life World" and will be used throughout.

The nascent self thus operates out of an ancient and species-specific *Umwelt* that has been honed and modified under conditions of stress and anxiety. It operates through instinct and has its connection to archetypes that form part of its living body. Even though the human *Umwelt* is fitted to our species it also has traits in common with other animal *Umwelten*, such as its reliance on signs and semiotic processes in general. With other animals we share the densely signifying sign processes of sexual selection, habitat creation, and adaptation to shifting environments. The demands of the *Umwelt* must be met before we can work out the role and location of our Horizons of meaning that are uniquely human.

For the nascent self, then, the human *Umwelt* guides its first 'take' on the world, that is, its first motor coordinations, its first sensory experiments with variable stimuli, and its complex response patterns to ever larger spheres of interaction. But even here on the most basic level of organism/environment transaction we have more going on than a simple stimulus response reflex event. The nascent self, even as an infant, does not merely eject a given response for a given stimulus. For one thing, there is no such thing as a 'pure' stimulus, as any input from the world will be embedded in a cluster of co-given stimuli events that help shape the very meaning and value of the 'isolated' stimulus. A loud sound will be registered, that is, interpreted, differently depending upon its surrounding noises or events. There is no such thing as "*the* loud noise as *the* stimulus." The noise is always *taken* as some noise in a context of expectation. For example, it could be 'heard' as a gunshot in one context and a carnival noise in another context. And all sounds, stimuli, exist in a larger order of information in which there is a signal-to-noise ratio that embeds the stimulus in noises that often make it hard to isolate and amplify the stimulus itself.

Responses can also shape the very meaning of the stimulus or stimuli. This is so from the simplest sensory observation to the structure of quantum events in physics. John Dewey gives a concise phenomenological description of how an infant coordinates its responses to a lit candle by a series of feedback loops, each of which is a mini adjustment to what had just been done before. He destroys the idea that the so-called reflex arc is a simple dyadic event of stimulus → response with nothing happening in between. The fact of the matter is that the between space, namely where the organism (infant) is actually perceiving and acting, is quite active in shaping the immediacy of the external raw sense data input into stabilized physical object events over which the nascent self has some mastery or at least self-protective awareness (Dewey 1896).

The limitations of classical drive theory are especially evident when we engage in an ordinal phenomenological account of how the nascent self develops its own ontology on its way to fulfilling the selving process. The key here is to note that there is a direct and necessary parallel between the ontology of the self and the ontology of the objects with which the self interacts. One can only separate the two ontologies by an act of what Peirce called "prescinding" that lifts the object of study out of its natural habitat to see it in isolation. Once this is done it is necessary to reinsert the phenomenon back into its larger context and weave it into the whole from which it was prescinded. Needless to say, this process requires skill and patience but it is exactly what the method of ordinal phenomenology has been designed to do, that is, to describe phenomena as they are located in larger ordinal locations and then examine the subaltern locations of the relevant phenomena. The phenomena of the selving process are best seen and described in terms of their ordinal locations: personal, communal, religious, and aesthetic.

The nascent self needs what has been called (Kohut) self-objects in its life that give it some healthy narcissistic identity as a self that matters and has value in the world. The self-object is a special kind of object that ontologically distinctive, that, is, it is not like other objects in the world. The self-object straddles the difference between objectness, as thing like, and consciousness, as self like. The parents, or their analogues, function as the self-objects by the ways they empower the nascent self to have more power of being and to find its place in the world of intense competition and compulsive interaction. Thus one can say that ontologically there are three kinds of 'things' in the inventory of the world: (1) objects, (2) selves, and (3) self-objects. While this ontology lacks philosophical sophistication it serves pragmatically to show how the self evolves with its self-objects to become more fully open to the selving process that is one of nature's greatest accomplishments and yet deepest mysteries.

For Kohut, psychoanalysis can help affect a cure for the struggling adult self as it works hard to find the inner strength to build a healthy narcissism that can fill in the abyss left by non-empathic parents who were too involved with their own unfulfilled narcissistic needs to help their child develop along healthy channels. For Kohut:

> The conceptualization of a pathology of the self leads in these cases to the recognition that the patient's resistance against being analytically penetrated is a healthy force, preserving the existence of a rudiment of a nuclear self that had been established despite the parents' distorted empathy; it also leads to the recognition that this nuclear self is becoming increasingly reactivated, i.e., the analyst witnesses the revival of the analysand's archaic conviction of the greatness of his self—a conviction that had remained unresponded to in early life and had thus not been available for gradual modification and integra-

tion with the rest of the personality; and, finally, it leads to the recognition that a working-through process is being mobilized which concerns the claims of the reactivated nuclear self in one (or several) of a self-object transference. This working-through process begins in most instances with the mobilization of archaic needs for mirroring and for merger; as working through is maintained, it gradually transforms the patient's ideas of archaic greatness and his wishes for merger with the omnipotent objects into healthy self-esteem and wholesome devotion to ideals. (Kohut 1977: 149–150)

Through the transference relationship to the analyst, or to any other significant figure, text, or event, the analysand can reignite the nascent self to flower in fullness even if at the beginning of the process there will be, as per necessity, some psychic inflation. This grandiosity is necessary just from an energetic standpoint if the self is to make a dramatic move to push out from the cold realm of failed parenting into the warm realm of self love and self acceptance. The idealization of the transference object, that is, the belief that the self-object is perfect and all knowing, gives way to a healthy appraisal of its limits, which in turn provides the free space within which selving can once again move forward past and through the transference.

In all of these cases, the natural difference between *nature naturing* and *nature natured* is operating behind the scenes to empower and frame the selving process. The selving process is ultimately rooted in an awareness of the seemingly fitful momenta of the fissuring of the natural difference where the potencies of the unconscious of nature enter into the awareness of the self through the self-objects in its life. In this sense, then, the highly charged and important self-objects are the gateway to the unconscious of nature and the potencies that emerge from the dark fringes of consciousness. This relationship to the precious self-objects can be described in different but commensurate language frames.

In one mode of expression one can say that the self-object is partly submerged in the unconscious and partly in the conscious worlds of parental interaction. Note that the self-object need not be confined to one's parents or parental substitutes, but could actually be an 'object' that is not human yet which has tremendous semiotic power such as a sacred text or meaningful work of art. The self-object is rich in meaning because it has the unique quality of reaching into the depths of the various layers of the unconscious. The greater the self-object's potency, the deeper down into the unconscious it goes, with the greatest, those of works of genius, emerging from the depths of *nature's* unconscious as well as the 'upper' layers of the collective and personal unconscious. Traditional self-object theory confines this ontological category to the human parents, while ordinal psychoanalysis opens out the deeper and broader ordinal locations in which the pre-human forms of the self-object also appear to phenomenological insight. Ordinal psychoanalysis refuses to rest in the narrow realm of the intra-psychic or even the inter-subjective, but moves into the fuller domain where psyche and world inter-connect on all ontological levels and all relevant ordinal locations. Ordinal phenomenology is the method or means by which these ordinal locations can be made transparent to enlightened query. The discipline of ontological parity keeps phenomenology open to all varieties of self-objects regardless of their whence or whither, while the focus on traits rather than essences prevents query from a premature collapse into the fixed and falsely certain.

In this broadened ontology of the self-object we can see how special non-human orders (complexes) can serve in this unique capacity of holding open the natural difference for the emerging self-in-process. Such objects, for example, as noted, a sacred text, a history of (claimed) revelation, a powerful narrative, a great work of art, a world changing personality, a broadening scientific vista, or anything that opens out the potencies of nature as appearing within key orders of the world (*nature natured*), make it possible for the individual to stand astride the natural difference and keep both sides of the great fissuring open, if only briefly. Again, while classical psychoanalysis, as revised by Kohut, would confine the self-object to the human order, ordinal psychoanalysis makes the ontological claim that self-objects can also be found in the non-human realms of nature insofar as those realms become transparent to the primacy of the natural difference; namely, the perennial fissuring that is the primal *way* of nature. Transitional objects, such as a favorite blanket or teddy bear, are here understood to be self-objects in that they dip down into a field of meaning that touches the underground currents of the unconscious of nature. They are overcharged with meaning in just the right way as to give the nascent self connection to pre and post-human orders of meaning, with the "posthuman" here being defined as the realm of religious transcendence, but a transcendence that is always within the one nature that there is. And, as we shall see in chapter 4, this religious transcendence will itself be rooted in a deeper layer, that of the aesthetic sublime.

The nascent self has now left the alleged supremacy of the erogenous zones behind and may or may not have negotiated the Oedipal constellation, which at best is a finite historical complex and not universally instantiated. For a self-psychology the issue is not that of castration anxiety in most cases but the struggle to develop a unified image of an autonomous self that is sustained in its growth trajectory by a healthy parental mirroring and idealization that provides it with its own legitimate narcissism, that is, its sense of self-worth and value that comes from parental love and affirmation. When this affirmation is not present the self falls backward into a fragmented sense of being partitioned and not whole and may be reduced to a creature of the drives and their concretization in the erogenous zones.

Two modes of pathology converge at this early stage of the selving process—roughly during the latency period and into adolescence. We can use two theoretical frames to describe the same thing, one being the language of self-object and the other being the language of orgonotics. Note again that the ontology of the self-object has been broadened beyond Kohut's formulation. Reich's orgone biophysics is here slightly deliteralized but held to be theoretically important and useful nonetheless.

At one extreme you have the situation where nothing, human or not, can emerge as a self-object. That is, there is a flattening of affect and ideation such that the individual cannot distinguish between a human complex, say, a face, and a non-human complex. This is seen in some forms of autism. There are no specially marked orders that do what the self-object is supposed to do; namely, to open out the unconscious of nature while at the same time holding the nascent selving process secure in its openness to the abyss beneath its consciousness. More common is the recoil from the abyss of nature's unconscious that shuts down the opening potency of the self-object and flattens out the ontology of the self-object so that it sinks back down into the status of being just a 'safe' object among others. There is an anxiety of being that the self will do almost anything to wash away by stripping the self-object of its depth-dimension. In essence, the self settles for less being in order to avoid the demands of more being, a heightening of being that is a gift to the self from the self-object. For example, a sacred text, as a self-object, may demand of us that we change our life, but we experience increased anxiety in hearing that call so we flatten out the text into a series of historical documents that are not binding on us today, or we convert everything to metaphor and see the text as a kind of literature for the less well educated. Whatever strategy we chose the goal is the same, to close off the selving process from the growth prospects that require courage in the face of anxiety and the new.

Parallel to this description of how pathology works its way into the self-object relations is Reich's notion of the armor rings that encircle the body and that freeze energy in segments that hold onto their energy charges but are forced to channel them in neurotic ways. As noted, Reich believes that the core energy of the human process is positive and that there is nothing neurotic built-into the primal sexual energy that we are and embody. Under the ancient conditions of matriarchy all sexual relations were open and fluid and there were no Oedipal complexes and, hence, no castration anxiety existed within the extended families of the social groups constituting matriarchal society. The complexes and neuroses that Freud describes as constitutive of life are actually products of patriarchy and simply will cease to exist once matriarchy is reestablished through a liberation of sexual energy and what Reich called "work democracy."

Each of the armored rings encircles a specific part of the body, for example, there is a pelvic ring and an ocular ring. Behind these rings there is a massive energy charge of raw sexual energy that is pushing against the ring. As the internal pressure increases so too does the anxiety level. Neurosis occurs because the sexual energy must find a substitute outlet other than the appropriate and normal genital/orgasmic, which is blocked. The blockage comes from the personal and social super-ego, which operates unrelentingly to freeze up orgonotic streaming. Here is where the phobias and fetishes emerge, as products of re-cathected bio-sexual energy.

These rings must be addressed in turn. The strongest ring surrounds the pelvic floor and represents the seat of genital energy. Therapy includes physical touch of the armored segments in an attempt to loosen up the musculature that is holding the orgone energy back in real and metaphorical knots. When the armoring is pierced there is a dramatic release of emotion and energy, often accompanied by memories of childhood abuse, but not necessarily so. Reich was far less interested in patient's memories or dreams than he was in their orgonotic energy dynamics.

Combining these two theoretical models we can say that the armored individual cannot cathect energy toward a proper self-object because the imperial super-ego has equated the desire toward the other tempting self with sin or, at least a kind of self-betrayal. Hence, the blocked energy must take an underground route toward a substitute object that, by definition, cannot be a full self-object, only a flattened out mockery of one. The armored self has no self-object in the full sense, although he or she will have at least more of a rudimentary sense than an autistic person will have. Armoring by its very nature works against the kinds of opening practiced by ordinal phenomenology. But knowing this makes it easier for this kind of phenomenology to sniff out the hiding places where armoring is born and does its work. As cannot be stated enough, ordinal phenomenology is not just a method of description of any and all relevant phenomena; it is also an ongoing spiritual discipline that helps the practicing phenomenologist become more authentic in her or his existence, and more attuned to the semiotic codes that permeate living systems, both conscious and unconscious.

The adolescent self seeks an autonomous identity that turns its back on its conditions of origin and struggles to open up a not-yet-being in the unrealized future that will find and instantiate an ideal self that is situated in the psyche as an ego ideal, a kind of positive version of the super ego. The ego ideal is itself a mobile self-object that has within its contour the power of the unconscious, as do all self-objects. This ideal is rotated toward the light of the *not yet*, toward an open and expanding future that beckons it onward toward a vision of wholeness that can't be replicated by anything that is a mere object within the vast infinity of *nature natured*.

For many, Reich's notion of a special ultra-refined non-electromagnetic orgone energy sounds like science fiction, and perhaps it is. Had he confined himself to a more metaphorical analysis of sexual energy and dynamics his legacy might have been brighter. However, when used more metaphorically his system has a stark clarity about it that is commendable and his social and political deconstructions of fascism are profound and brilliant as will come out in the next chapter. In what follows we will return to Schopenhauer's concept of the Will and rework the natural difference and the self-object theory, as they in turn correlate to the underground momentum of the ongoing birth trauma.

The selving process can also be seen in terms of the strenuous momenta of the Will to life as it surges through the human psyche and soma pushing the self out into personal and social space, personal and social time, and into the vast causal chains that permeate its life. We noted how the intelligible character is the basal figure for the self and exists just prior to the moment of the violent insertion into space, time, and causality—the source of the birth trauma. It must be stressed that for ordinal psychoanalysis the birth trauma is both a psychological and an ontological event. In the former sense it involves the transition from the womb to external unfriendly nature, while in the ontological sense it involves the leap from the pre-spatial, the pre-temporal, and the pre-causal, to the exploding world of full spatial, temporal, and causal relationships that extend without end, with neither beginning nor consummation—just endless repetition and continual cycling.

The Will has no mentality, no consciousness of itself *as* Will, and certainly no plan for the human species. In us it reaches its highest objectification or manifestation and it is only in us, in the known universe, that it becomes an object of consciousness, in this case initially through our sensations of its willing in our body. It makes no sense to call it god, or devil for that matter. It is just pure willing and nothing more. It can be blocked in armoring rings and misdirected in neuroses and can explode into manic episodes in bipolar disorder. The Will needs form in order to manifest itself yet it also shatters form where the particular form is too weak to sustain itself. For our purposes it is most pertinent to note that the Will to Life is the great unconscious of nature that pours itself into the human collective unconscious and its archetypes, and via that route into the personal unconscious and its feeling-toned complexes. The irony is that the Will is blind but it is what makes it possible for us to see into the heart of nature and its many depths. Ordinal phenomenology can trace its pathways in nature and describe its unfoldings within the world and human meaning horizons.

We remind ourselves that the concepts of Will, *nature naturing*, the material maternal, the lost object, and the unconscious of nature, are roughly equivalent. One usage is preferred over another only when a shift of emphasis is desired, say, one focusing on the *dynamism* of Will, or a focus on the *fecundity* of naturing, the *nurturing* of the womb/*chora*, the *melancholy* of the no longer, or the *darkness* of nature. Taken together these five concepts reinforce and enrich each other and belong in the Same (*das Selbst*), as Heidegger would put it. In the Same they all gather around the self-giving core of meaning that stands at the point of origin for what is located in the depths.

The Will is present in self-objects with a special intensity and binds the Will in those objects to the Will in the human subject. Intensity reaches out to intensity and they reinforce each other. This process is partly unconscious and reaches its strongest form in the psychoanalytic transference in which the analyst functions as the self-object for the analysand. Will speaks to itself although it appears as if there are two forces in relation. The classical philosophical conundrum of the one and the many may have its roots in the perennial experience we have of the Will, which is always one but almost always appears as at least two. For Schopenhauer, leaning on Hindu metaphysics, the Will is one alone and the 'experience' of its manyness is "maya" or illusion, a false consciousness that is a product of our ensnarement in space, time, and causality.

Pathology emerges whenever the self-in-process fails to honor the fissuring of the natural difference and tries to freeze the relevant self-object, whether human or not, into a static kind of thing that does not reach down into the unconscious depths of *nature naturing*. This flattened ontology, even in its more sophisticated form (the cat is on the mat) betrays the most fundamental difference within nature and isolates the self from its own depths, causing it to rotate around a deadened center of wooden habits that have minimal room for growth and transformation. This process takes hold in adulthood when habit begins to solidify into a massive structure of behavior that closes out novelty and any deep introspection into the unconscious, which is abjected by the attending consciousness. Rigidity and abjection go together, the former cutting off the movements that open to the material maternal and the latter tainting the lost object with a vile negativity that renders it odious. Abjection is an over-determined ongoing act that combines disgust with desire and fascination. Using traditional language we can say that the anal 'stage' involves an initial fascination with feces that evolves into an abjection that is learned, although it also has evolutionary roots from a health perspective. The abjection of the lost object, aka, the material maternal, has a tremendous propulsive force for moving the nascent self forward into the demanding and compelling orders of *nature natured*. Abjection is thus both necessary and tragic at the same time but in different respects.

Abjection is a necessity because it opens out the subject/object split with enough force to get consciousness pulling away from its unconscious ground. It must be remembered that the unconscious of nature has a tremendous power when contrasted to the fragile sphere of finite human consciousness. Nascent consciousness almost needs a push, as it were, to stand up on its own shaky legs and this push comes from the momentum of abjection that recoils against the powers of the unconscious. Without the recoil of abjection consciousness would never have the energy or audacity to emerge in the first place. But consciousness always comes at a price and that price is that it must turn against the dark matrix from which it comes, struggling to shove its powers and potencies underground and out of sight, and it is precisely the role that abjection takes on in intra-personal growth and evolution. We will examine communal abjections in the next chapter and see how abjection operates inter-subjectively to prop up various forms of pathological social life.

But abjection is not a once-and-for-all event but a primal momentum that undergirds all conscious existence, making room for an ever-expanding consciousness. Abjection is what Hegel would call a moment of "negativity" that pushes a shape of self-awareness into its opposite so that the dialectic of an expanding spirit can continue to grow indefinitely toward an absolute knowing—the attainment of philosophy. Abjection is negation but it is more complex than a simple denial because it contains the desire for the negated object and simultaneously suppresses that very desire. The classical Freudian concept of ambivalence captures the logic of abjection fairly well.

Abjection becomes tragic if it is not examined in its inner logic and seen to be *over* determined in its sway within the personal and/or social psyche. It initially needs to be an over the top force just to help consciousness leap free from the powers of origin in the unconscious of nature. The inertial power of the unconscious is greater than nascent consciousness can imagine. The sheer energy needed to enter the zone of detached awareness must be greater than the feeble powers of nascent consciousness. Selving could not get launched without abjection. Hence the force of abjection pushes consciousness too far away from the unconscious of nature because there is no other way to pry consciousness loose from the conditions of origin. The possibility of the tragic enters here because consciousness may not be able to reweave its own powers with the unconscious of nature because the abjection worked all too well.

Consciousness can become convinced that there are no unconscious potencies to encounter, that only *nature natured* exists, under whatever name, and that it is master in its own house. It sees itself as free-floating and autonomous, nature's most prized product, originating in itself and choosing its own telos in a life filled with innumerable options, all equally available. Consciousness, in this detached and unaware state, believes in its free will and mocks any effort to show it the potencies and powers resident in seeing both sides of the natural difference; namely, in the eternal fissuring of *nature naturing* ejecting/birthing *nature natured*.

Schopenhauer argued that consciousness was always deluded into thinking it had the ability to freely choose among several options for pending behavior. From its perspective, consciousness weighs a set of options of equal psychic weight and value before choosing the one that is most desirable for its flourishing. It is a freely made choice among genuinely equal possibilities. What is in fact happening is that the Will has pushed one option to the surface and the self is compelled to pick it regardless and remains deluded into thinking it had selected it on its own merits. For Schopenhauer, consciousness has little if any freedom in the face of the imperial Will that shapes and governs what it 'decides.' The only freedom that emerges for the finite conscious mind is in the domain of art and genius, and, more deeply, in the radical denial of the Will, as we have noted. In the last chapter we will transform and invert Schopenhauer's model by showing how the aesthetic sublime is the highest goal reachable by the selving process as it moves beyond the religious sphere to the domain of art, thus also inverting Kierkegaard's model, which elevates the religious over the ethical and the ethical over the aesthetic, but can only do so by creating a caricature of the domain of the arts and the aesthetic that reduces them to the sensual and narcissistic.

Identity formation in adulthood is highly shaped and grooved by habit, that "great flywheel of society" in the words of William James. The core of the self-image comes from the ego ideal that serves as a, hopefully, positive version of the super ego; namely, as a measure of the outward social attainment of existential potency within the relevant social orders of the mature and effective self. This ego ideal lives in the draft of the not-yet-being that holds it open to further growth and possible fulfillment. Each self has the prospect of living out of a potentially open future in which its own ancient habits have the prospect of becoming slightly more fluid and responsive to novel situations. In the third chapter we will examine in detail the process of "god-ing" in which extra-human, but not extra-natural, energies enter into the selving process at certain key junctures helping it to evolve in more decidedly creative ways. God-ing is not *a* or *the* god in a theistic or even panentheistic sense, but is a potency within nature that has a special relationship to the heart of human evolution. In encountering god-ing energies the self can evolve in striking ways, yet always consistent with the principles of the Neo-Darwinian synthesis. In other words, the entwinement of god-ing and selving does not entail a violation of the principles of natural selection or random variation.

In the long arc from the intelligible character, to the state of dreaming innocence, to the nascent infant self, to the emergent sign-using self, to adolescence and adulthood where sign systems become highly communal and complex, to the eventual decline in powers and death, selving retains its ancient and urgent features for the self-in-process. Internal and external semiosis concretize

the selving process and leave traces of nature that form the body
of the self's identity through time. The human process is semiotic
through and through but not exhaustively so. And it is important
to stress that human sign systems are as ancient as the species
itself having served our species well for millions of years. However it does not follow that all human sign systems are benign or
helpful for our survival let alone thriving. Critical common sense
uses those ancient signs that retain evolutionary value in current
adaptations, while, hopefully, critiquing and rejecting those signs
and systems that constitute maladaptations in our current meaning horizons. Further, pathological signs and powers continue to
punctuate the selving process rendering it unstable and often at
war with itself. The self is frequently split between pragmatically
useful and pathologically destructive signs pulling in opposite directions. Sign systems have vector force and power, they are not
airy nothings that float into and out of consciousness but energies
and directions that push and pull as well as illuminate and guide.

As we make our transition from personal selving to communal
forms of the selving processes, semiotics becomes more important. We are the sign making and sign using animals and we spend
our existence swimming in vast streams of semiosis whose origins
and goals are out of the range of even our most robust forms of
vision. Signs take on a life of their own and act independently
from given sign users although not from all sign users. It is tempting, and a form of narcissism, to see signs as purely personal
subjective products that only exist within human subjects who
create them to render the complexity of experience more manageable. Current philosophical prejudice avers that sign making is
primary while the assimilation of extra-personal signs is really an
illusion stemming from a temporary lack of knowledge of the
actual subjective origin of the signs in question. Put differently,
the manipulative dimension of semiosis is privileged over the as-
similative (Buchler) or the stress is on doing rather than undergo-

ing (Dewey). Put either way, half of semiosis is ignored if not abjected, that is, pushed aside as a threat to our imperial drive for detached autonomy where I remain the sign master and control the fate of the signs in my purview. *Class signing)*

But in a naturalistic perspective such as this one the stress falls equally on the dimension of assimilation or undergoing where the self receives signs it did not make and receives part of its meaning contour from these signs. Signs always come as part of series that give them shape and enhance their scope and density within semiosis. There is no such thing as a single sign for the simple reason that a sign is what it is by being a sign *of* something other than itself. Nor is there such a thing as a first sign, as argued by Peirce, as all signs are part of antecedent forms of semiosis that go back indefinitely into the mists of time. By the same token there will be no last sign as there will always be more to interpret, more to grasp, more to explore in and through signs. Semiosis permeates the innumerable orders of *nature natured* and serves to make communication and interaction possible for sign using creatures, whether human or not.

In our phenomenological descriptions of selving we have focused on the personal dimensions as they unfold longitudinally within the purview of ordinal psychoanalysis. Some brief communal aspects have been adumbrated where pertinent to the individual focus, especially around issues in psychopathology. In what follows in the next chapter we will continue the phenomenological description of selving but shift to the communal orders of interaction. The key here will be the multi-forms of semiosis as they relate to the self/community interface where the various social selves that weave themselves into and through the individual sign user become known with a fair degree of transparency. Social pathology will be examined using ordinal psychoanalysis; especially Reich's deconstruction of fascism and an outline of the prospects for a non-pathogenic social life will be proffered.

2

COMMUNAL VISTAS

The selving process is natively communal from its a priori structure in the intelligible character to its most sophisticated intersubjective symbolic forms (Cassirer 1929). The intelligible character is a species-specific pre-temporal, pre-spatial, and pre-causal form that connects all selves in a communal destiny that is the
proper for-having of species membership. The womb, cosmic and
biological, is the place and space for connection with universal
powers and structures that are part of shared communal energy
and trans-individual form. In fact, to talk of individual selving at
all is to prescind from the communal aspect of the larger selving
process. And while such prescinding is necessary, we must now
reweave the individual into its communal dimensions in the following phenomenological descriptions. Community exists in a bewildering variety of forms in the humanly occupied orders and we
will concentrate on the most important of these as they shape the
communal selving process for good and ill.

A major aspect of human community is its use of signs and
symbols for communication and articulation of its various horizons of meaning and structures of power. The discipline of semiotics, as founded by Peirce in the 1860s, has established that all
communication and all intellection takes place in and through

signs, from the simplest transaction such as a finger pointing to the moon (Zen Buddhism) to a sophisticated blueprint of a top secret submarine (Sherlock Holmes). In both cases, the sign points to something other than itself and enables the interpreter of the sign(s) to understand the nature of the referent of the sign. Peirce's simple triadic model better serves the phenomenological data than the dyadic model of post-structuralism. For Peirce we have a sign referring to an object that in turn produces what he calls an *interpretant,* which is a new sign emerging from the initial sign/object correlation. All signs refer to something other than themselves and all referents spawn an interpretant (new sign) that is then part of the expanding series of new interpretants. The current perspective (aesthetic naturalism) shares Peirce's semiotic realism; namely, the view that signs refer to objects that exist in a world that is independent of language and that these objects (natural complexes) generate an ongoing stream of new signs (interpretants) that can be explored indefinitely. Peirce's commitment to a pragmatic realism supports his semiotic theory and protects it from the subjective biases of its Continental cousins for whom signs refer only to other signs in a process of deferral and endless othering. That this latter model has ended in a dead end has slowly begun to be realized.

Our analysis of community will follow two different but commensurate tracks, one being the phenomenological description of its semiotic structures, with the second being a description and analysis of its psychoanalytic dynamics. As will become clear, ordinal phenomenology will uncover the myriad forms of semiosis within community, while ordinal psychoanalysis will disclose forms of pathology that haunt and distort collective living and association. These approaches are "commensurate" in that they are working on the same subject matter but from different foci, the former stressing the sign systems that envelop and shape communal vistas and the latter stressing the distortions of power and meaning that corrupt these sign systems. Normative analyses of positive forms of semiosis will be laid out in chapter 4, as will the psychoanalytic aspects of the creative aesthetic life (Rank 1930).

A semiotic approach to the human self is now well established and has reached a high degree of sophistication. But there have been few efforts to unite a semiotic with a psychoanalytic approach (Muller & Brent 2000). Specifically, there has been no work using the psychoanalytic theories of Reich, Jung, and Rank, to augment the theories of Freud. In the previous chapter this work was begun and in this chapter it will continue on the explicitly communal level. At the same time, *ordinal* psychoanalysis will continue to develop its own categories as it struggles with the data-field of its explorations into normal and pathological communal life. The most exciting prospects for communal selving lie in the domains of the multi-layered semiotic unconscious that both spawns and devours signs and sign systems. One of the goals of ordinal psychoanalysis, as allied with ordinal phenomenology, is to provide a partial road map of the unconscious, both of the self, and, ultimately, of nature. But this latter portrayal will only be accomplished at the conclusion of our research after painstaking and careful descriptions have also been made of communal, religious, and aesthetic modes of semiosis.

Thus we begin with the recognition that the human process is semiotic through and through and that it traffics in signs from the very beginning of its brief trajectory in the domain of space, time, and causality. However, at first it is like an animal in its *Umwelt*; namely, it uses signs but doesn't yet know that they *are* signs. The good breast is world, not a sign of it, not yet a sign of the material maternal as the receding ground of the self-in-process (Kristeva 1974). The nipple is the place where being is concentrated, the locus of the power of being as it infuses the nascent self with its unambiguous plenitude—the one of which there is no other. The self is neither personal nor communal, neither an agent of action nor a presence to itself. It is awash in what Peirce called "first-ness," that is, pure feeling and pure immediacy without any "sec-ondness" or dyadic otherness, just thereness. Or, to put it differ-ently, the nascent self is pure potentiality with only the barest minimum of actuality. It awaits the quickening touch of both form and the sense of otherness, made possible by abjection and an innate drive of self-othering, as described in the previous chap-ter.

The focus in this chapter is on the communal or horizontal aspects of how the selving process simultaneously moves laterally into semiotic streams and currents that are ancient and compel-ling. The first thing to note is that signs never occur singly but are always part of one or more series whose beginnings are shrouded in mist. Peirce argued decisively that there cannot be a first sign as there cannot be an absolute origin for anything in the pluri-verse of signs and objects. We can fasten on a sign and call it an original or first sign for specific interpretive reasons but this is a violent act that rips the sign out of its semiotic field of operation. A pragmatic decision to start somewhere *within* a sign series may be necessary but it must always be understood that it is arbitrary.

The human process, then, is permeated with innumerable sign series that it did not create. Nor does the self know in a conscious and thematic way just what sign series belong to it even if they may be partly transparent when the self is compelled to examine them under a situation where they may be under attack or at least questioned as to their validity. For the most part, one's sign sys-tems run along reasonably well until a contradiction between or among two or more of them surfaces in a minor or major crisis in which the self is forced to confront incompatible sign systems with conflicting claims and demands. Before the crisis the semiot-ic system bumped along reasonably well without a noticeable con-flict but when conditions changed, either internally or externally, the truce could no longer be maintained and the community of sign systems was broken or torn. The sign using self was forced to confront its split integrity.

When dealing with the *metaphysics* of community, that is, with the most generic and pervasive of its features, a certain stretch of vision is called for and the ability to let go of common paradigms is required. One of the most common misconceptions is that membership in a community requires conscious assent and the direct awareness of at least some of the other members of the said community. But this applies only to certain types of advanced community. The metaphysical minimum for a human community is that two or more persons have one or more perceived natural complexes in common (Buchler). They need not be aware of each other, nor need they be thematically aware of the complexes held in common. On this understanding, persons occupy numerous communities beyond their conscious awareness but they have effects after all; they matter and shape the ongoing life of experience and contrivance. Often an unconscious communal affiliation (some complex experienced and held in common) will suddenly become conscious and dramatically insistent in its thereness, its ineluctable presence as a complex that now directly shapes a community however small in scope. Most of our community affiliations are of this unconscious kind and there is the moral issue surrounding the fact that they are not fully consistent with each other. Many moral dilemmas stem from the ontic fact that each person maintains incompatible value commitments as allied to different sub-communities within the over arching selving process. While it might seem a worthy goal to bring unity into all subaltern value systems, it is not only impossible in principle, but its attainment would actually and ironically freeze out the genuine ambiguity that obtains in the world itself. Not only is a total harmony of values impossible in principle, given the ordinal nature of the world, it is not desirable especially as it would deaden contrast and the energy that comes from creative conflict.

As noted, one especially compelling way to approach the issue of community is through semiotics, the systematic study of those items in nature that signify in some respect, that is, point beyond themselves to a natural complex that is in turn rendered as a sign of something beyond its self, and so on indefinitely. It is as if signs have a hunger to belong to series of endlessly expanding scope and for each series itself to intersect with other series. The human process, via the inner dynamics of selving, is what it is because of the infinitizing potencies of innumerable sign systems that permeate it and carry it forward into larger and larger orders of the world. This is not to say that the self is a helpless plaything of infinite semiosis, although from the perspective of aesthetic naturalism much of it is determined and so shaped, but to illuminate the fact that we inherit the meaning horizons that enable us to have a world horizon at all. We tend to forget the long and complex processes that we have undergone to assimilate and then activate these ancient sign systems so as to give us our full meaning horizons. Beyond that, we fail to recognize that we actually *have* a horizon and rather assume that we are simply open to reality per se, not, in fact, a partly subjectively framed dimension of it.

It helps here if we think of sign series as living organisms that have life cycles and life energies—meaning this metaphorically but importantly. There are no first or last signs. Pragmatic semiotics, other than Peirce, eschews any eschatology that would insist that there will be the final interpretant or a/the last sign. We are always *in medias res* with the origin or the goal forever shrouded in thick mist by the very nature of things, that is, not to any failing on our part as interpreters. Peirce and Royce can rescue us from our blindness by means of a cosmic semiotician for whom all that is first and all that is last is known, just not known by us. Royce's model of absolute semiosis is complete in its structure and details whereas Peirce's notion of the absolute remains truncated and fragmentary—vaguely Neo-Platonic and in part derived from Schelling.

Each sign system is a community in its own right and as such can include or exclude potential new members. When a self encounters another self the first thing that happens is that one or more sign series are lit up and present the new self to the first self and, of course, vice versa. Note that this process is for the most part routine and without a high anxiety level, partly because of the ubiquity of what Jung called the "persona," which is the outward mask that we wear that presents a socially viable self to others. It puts us into a type (genus) such as a profession or political affiliation, while masking the deeper alliances or subaltern communal commitments that may prevail within the psyche. Without the persona leading the way, social congress would be profoundly fractious and unstable, if not a war of all against all, certainly a raw and torturous affair with little or no convergence of semiotic systems and content.

Personal selving traffics in vast sign systems as it moves from the pre-temporal, pre-spatial, and pre-causal intelligible character toward an engagement with the most pervasive orders of *nature natured*, orders rendered into the great semiotic triad of sign → object → interpretant. These sign series help make the personal self what it is; namely, a unique moment in the history of world semiosis, that is unique in at least one respect that can be measured and gauged semiotically. But these same sign series are also, and more importantly, communal in nature and upshot, moving the selving process into the full panoply of social semiosis where purely private meanings often must give way before socially compelling publically available meanings. The selving process transmutes vast semiotic currents into personalized sign systems that give it its inner texture and outer contour that is partly available for public appraisal by the community of sign users.

There is a great deal of inertia in the public codes and sign systems that determine both ideation and behavior in human communities. Plasticity is rather quickly drained out of the system as habits reinforce repetition and cyclical reiteration—a kind of bad infinite of endless recurrence of old being. Inertial drift marks most instances of the human process and grooves and shapes the internal and external aspects of the selving process. Habit retraces its weary steps over and over again, rarely allowing for a fresh path across the horizonal landscape, almost never letting go of its economy of scarcity. It takes a sudden, or accumulated, rush of semiotic potency or energy to break through inertial habits that are millennia old, indeed, perhaps millions of years old. That this does in fact happen is a striking testament to the deep inner resources of the selving process, especially in the aesthetic powers of its most intensely enlightened mode of being as is manifest in the place where religious ideation sublates itself to give birth to redeeming art (Corrington 2010).

Thus a given sign (an abstraction) is embedded in at least one sign system, probably many more, and is part of an endless series of complex intersections and actual and potential ramifications. The branching process is promiscuous and fully natural. Serial intersection is inevitable and protean, although there are built-in limitations determining the scope and type of intersection. Not all intersections are com-possible in the same semiosphere, that is, one sign system may negate a piece or segment of another if they are brought into contact. It is important to understand that sign systems act like living organisms, as noted above, and that as such, they have territorial imperatives and needs. There simply is no such thing as Leibniz's pre-established harmony in the semiosphere. His own implied (and partly stated) semiotic theory fails to account for the actual travail undergone in semiotic competition. Natural selection goes all the way down.

These various sign series, in their semiotic thickness, form an actual infinite that grows and contracts as humans move in, out, around, and through them. There is a sense in which they obtain independently of any given sign user but perhaps not of all sign users. Their ontological status is profoundly interesting in that the actual infinite of signs is somehow larger in scope than the sum total of the signs currently housed in human and animal selves. This has led to some philosophers to speculate that there must be a cosmic mind that can contain all actual and possible signs in an atemporal 'moment' of vision in which finite minds can participate through analogy or some kind of mirroring process. Josiah Royce used the analogy of mapping in which one is asked to draw a perfect map of England while standing in the middle of England when doing the actual drawing. This new map is now a part of England and so it must be mapped as well. But, of course, this second map is also now a part of England and so must be drawn within the previous map. This produces an endless process of self-representation in which any one map that one chooses to extract from the series is a perfect image of the entire series, hence of England itself. The semiotic infinite, for Royce, is a perfect self-representative series of all of reality and finite minds have access to the Absolute via any finite entry point they chose within the reiterated series of maps. For the finite semiotic agent the Absolute is available to it through the radiant plenitude of the actual, indeed, actualizing infinite.

Need one posit an available Absolute sign container/creator in order to explain the nature of the actual infinite of semiosis that envelopes the finite sign user? This rather extreme conclusion can be avoided if one accepts the idea that sign systems can have a kind of inertial momentum of their own that allows for sign linkages that occur naturally within the sign series even if an attending human consciousness is not involved. This sounds like a species of crypto-idealism or another form of panpsychism (panexperientialism) wherein internal mentality can guide the sign series to augment its stock of signs through a muted consciousness or awareness that 'knows' what the new signs are and that they belong with the series. The conception I am working toward is at once simpler and more prosaic. A new sign 'joins' an actual/actualizing infinite series if its penumbra of meanings is commensurate with the contour of other signs in that series—a simple kind of iconic isomorphism, that is, a likeness drawn to a likeness. On another level, that of secondness, bare causal impaction, a new sign can join the series under discussion because it shares in the causal nexus of an antecedent sign from the pertinent actual infinite. Symbolicity (thirdness) works the same way; namely, through an isomorphism of generic content where likeness attracts likeness all to enhance the scope of the infinitizing of the actual infinite.

These phenomenological observations are designed to show that sign series form into communities of actualizing infinities that surround and interpenetrate the selving process and make human congress with the Other possible, not to mention the of-times bewildering worlds of internal semiosis. We are communal beings because we are semiotic beings and we need to grasp the nature of signs and their promiscuous series before we can understand the other structures of communal life. For Peirce, we are creatures with a "glassy essence" who can only come to know ourselves through our contrast with our social being, which we introject and make into our personal self. That is, the social self is the 'real' self, while the inner life is an echo of that larger and more important self. Peirce obviously overstates the case for the social self but he understood the nature of semiosis in shaping both dimensions of the human process. He also used the image of us as being (or containing) a "bottomless lake" which contains

To be is to be in an Economy

underwater "skeleton sets" of sign series that are already linked together in the unconscious. The lake is our unconscious self that has its own semiotic structures and powers that affect what goes on in the above water zone. Peirce was profoundly conflicted about the idea of a semiotic unconscious but he was willing to give a place to it in his vast cosmic system. I have argued that he abjected the unconscious in general and was ambivalent about firstness, especially about the role of firstness in the life of the psyche (Corrington 1993).

The selving process negotiates its way within the full scope, pressures, and invitations of the actual infinite of ongoing semiosis. Its social life is the life of social signs and these signs continue to shape and determine what is and what is not possible for the arc of the self through time. The actual infinite of signs (interpretants) is always actualiz*ing*, that is, it is always affecting and making semiotic space for itself by lighting up an ongoing series of interpretations of the object sphere under its purview. The self in its selving rides along with the actualizing series and is gathered into its delivered meanings as they collectively present a horizon of intelligibility. Selving is actualizing. Actualizing is empowering selving to flesh out its world and give it contour and depth. In the movement of semiosis the human process becomes clothed with the rich tapestry of meanings that are given to it by the actualizing infinite. To be a self is to be a locus for the mobile infinite of signs, but as rendered perspectively.

But this semiotic process is not one directional; namely from the actualizing infinite to the self. The self puts its own stamp, however minimal in most cases, onto the actualizing infinite. The power relation is asymmetrical. The vast networks of semiosis, that is, of unending sign series (endless interpretants), eclipse the powers of finite sign users either singly or collectively, and the individual has limited resources to alter the basic contours of the sign series that have surrounded and permeated it, since birth, if not before. As noted in the previous chapter, the individual thinks that it has more freedom of the will than it does. The metaphysical Will, that is, the depth Will of nature, surges forward and quickens our sign systems and empowers them to actualize themselves especially under the conditions of life, where one can equate Will with the *Will to Life*. This foundational (metaphysical) Will can, on a rare occasion, generate enough surplus charge to lift the self above the power of its regnant sign series and hold open a free space for creative and novel semiosis. In this sense there is the genuine prospect of free will on a limited scale, but it truly is free for a brief but important moment of time and leaves traces of its free movement on the rest of the structures and powers of the self. The selving process, in its communal semiotic dimensions, doesn't need a lot of free will in order to transform its prospects for personal and social betterment. A small surplus amount can illuminate vast stretches of the actualizing infinite and give it a novel set of meanings that it had not heretofore had.

A more complex sense of community emerges when two or more interpreters are not only conscious of some important orders (natural complexes) held in common, but are aware of each other and aware of each other being aware of each other—thus giving rise to double reflexivity. This quickly enriches the prospects for the instantiating of the actual infinite of mobile interpretants. Intersubjectivity is constituted by, among other things, serial intersection of sign systems from one or more subjects to another. The fecundity of each sign system determines the reach and depth of intersubjectivity making for a rich and complex series of ongoing intersections.

Intersubjectivity operates on many levels from the base tones of a rumbling unconscious to the complex higher tonalities of a multi-layered consciousness. In the former case, intersubjectivity represents the linkage of pre-thematized unconscious contents, perhaps pathological, and this conjoining of depth dimensions can have a tremendous, if unrecognized, effect of the rest of the psyche. In the latter case, consciousness can be enriched and challenged to augment and critique its own semiotic stock. Intersubjectivity is semiotic through and through. Signs and interpretants constitute its material body and it expands and contracts under environing (evolutionary) pressures. When one self, in its selving process, confronts or simply encounters, another, vast semiotic sign systems swing into action and frame the nascent relationality along highly routinized and usually predictable patterns. However, the interaction may loosen unexpected signs and interpretants from both interpreters or even generate new interpretants from the encounter. Intersubjectivity can be the locus of semiotic growth as well as be the locus of bland repetition and blind reiteration.

Peirce argues that the inner self is a product of social contrast in which external and competing sign series mark out the parameters of the personal subjective self. Contrast is necessary to give shape and texture to the sign-using interpreter as it negotiates its way around the complex semiosphere of its various communities. Not only must the nascent selving process wrestle with human communities (always more than one), but it must also deal with nature itself, which can also be seen as being constituted by communities of interaction. While nature is not a "community of communities," it harbors an astonishing array of communities 'within' it and the human process must learn which ones are pertinent to its survival and flourishing, not to mention which one needs to be protected in their own right. Aesthetic naturalism is committed to a strong ecological framework that affirms the intrinsic worth of non-human species.

Hegel describes the master slave dialectic in which one subjectivity tries to conquer another through a kind of reduction of its subjectivity to the lower status of being an object or a means to an end. The current perspective puts it differently. When two selves encounter each other their regnant (most pertinent and powerful) sign series, as part of the actualizing infinite, seek each other out through a kind of semiotic probe that finds its counterpart in the other self's sign series. Series speaks to series as the attending consciousnesses watch the process. This is to a large extent more of a passive process than the self will admit, as it is unaware of how sign series work "on their own" to link selves to the world and to each other. The contact between and among selves is through sign series and serial intersection. Quite rapidly, often based on the subtlest of visual or emotional cues and clues, the selves will feel out each other's semiotic parameters and will know the basic lay of the landscape of interpretants. This process has had to become fast and sure for obvious evolutionary reasons. So, inter-subjectivity could be better described as interhorizonality in which one complex semiotic horizon intersects with another, sometimes under great evolutionary pressure and sometimes in the luxury of a kind of semiotic play and *jouissance*.

The selving process thus operates in and through semiotic intersection and its task of maintaining semiotic harmonies is a great one. Process theologies quite rightly place a high value on the relationship between contrast and harmony arguing that the greatest (aesthetic) state maximizes contrast under harmonic con-ditions. The individual self must do this for its inner (intrahorizo-nal) sign series, for its interhorizonal sign series, and for the innu-merable sign series of *nature natured*. Without habit and semiotic inheritance these tasks would be impossible. Habit must be partly seen as in the honorific category as it is also the deposit of ancient (successful) evolutionary adaptations that, conditions being the same, can continue to guide the self in its semiotic transactions. Pragmatic perspectives such as this one balance the hermeneutics of suspicion with a judicious use of critical common sensism when talking about right use of method in probing into how habits work in shaping our interactions with the world.

At this juncture, and before we shift to the ordinal psychoanalytic account of community, it is pertinent to deal with two distinct types of communities (interhorizonality); namely, natural and interpretive. These communities are usually found together although the natural form is by far the more common and has great inertial mass and power. Communities of interpretation can only exist *within* natural communities and only under somewhat rare conditions. They are more fragile yet more valuable for species evolution.

We always find ourselves in natural communities that give us the basic semiotic parameters of our being-in-the-world. Such communities hark back to the conditions of origin, to our "whatness" in terms of race, class, gender, language, religion, aesthetic, and all conditions of "origin." Natural communities give us our full semiotic inheritance; our actual infinite of already attained signs, our living body of semiosis, our thickness and sheer thereness as interpreters. Such sign systems as we have add up to our collective identity and membership in our tribe. This membership is exclusivistic and primal. It functions quietly and smoothly for the most part, giving us stability and a kind of semiotic warmth that protects us from the threat of meaninglessness and despair. Our natural communities are inert and locked in place—they reiterate the vast ancient conditions of origin, the laws and rules of membership that exclude all non-tribal selves and which does so through a powerful demonization and abjection of Otherness.

Natural communities are jealous of their semiotic stock and deeply suspicious of any actual infinite that comes from outside of its own conditions of origin. There is little or no room for hermeneutics in a natural community as all signs and interpretants come pre-interpreted by the sovereign community itself. This can be done through a leader and his or her coterie or by the inertial mass of the sign systems themselves, or more usually by both. Any attempt at a novel reading of a specific sign series is quickly suppressed and the approved or stock reading is reinforced by power. Natural communities are ubiquitous in our species and are tied to antecedent sign series. Yet such communities can also become eschatological when they project their sign systems onto a future that, it is maintained, will fulfill the signs in its current depository of signs. The issue of eschatology is a complex one and will be dealt with when we deal with the pathology within communal life.

Natural communities use power to govern the flow of interpretants so that they have a minimal degree of novelty, rarely enhancing or modifying their antecedent signs and certainly not expanding in the direction of new meaning. Here we can talk of controlled and flattened interpretants that are hardly interpretants at all. They are so only in the sense that they are additions to the sign series of which they are a part, but there is almost total inertia in their trajectory through time. We say that a sign interpreted is a sign changed or conversely that a sign changed is a sign interpreted, but this logic just barely holds in a natural community that sees open hermeneutics as the enemy insofar as it insists that each interpretant stream becomes available for ramified probing and analysis, that is, for spawning new and novel interpretants. And while the degree of novelty is rarely great it is still there when the right kind of communal life allows for the unfolding of creatively contrived interpretants.

In contrast to these ubiquitous natural communities, which occupy most of our semiotic lives, are the communities of interpretation that have a very different relationship to signs and interpretants. These communities do not exist alone in some kind of free floating sphere but grow out of, yet remain within, natural communities. We are never free from natural communities, but communities of interpretation come and go based on a set of conditions within natural communities that make them possible however briefly. The main requirement is that there needs to be a certain quantum of surplus energy left over after all instrumental needs have been met by a sufficient number of members of a given natural community. Evolutionary competence requires huge sums of energy in rendering the organism/environment (interpreter/nature) relationship stable and fully adaptive over the life expectancy of the individual selving process. This applies to the social group in the same way and to the social aspect of selving. If the basic needs of interpreters and agents are met and the surplus energy is freely under some kind of personal and social control, then the hermeneutic processes can begin to realign energies in search for novel and creative interpretants—the world can be lit up in new ways.

A nascent community of interpreters will start locally to pry selected signs free from their deadened sign cluster and hold them up to the light of circumspective vision. In this gesture room is instantly created for novel and enriched interpretants to unfold from the original signs. New signs bloom and old signs take on new meanings as the flow of interpretants increases along new pathways. Suddenly interpreters realize that the 'official' interpretation of a particular sign series is not only ad hoc and arbitrary but may also have demonic and corrupt elements. This realization gives birth to a felt need for the creation of a new model of interpretation; namely, a hermeneutics of suspicion. Not only does the new community of interpreters generate and experience novel interpretants, it also has eyes to see the various distortions imposed on sign series by the monolithic natural community.

If natural communities have at their extreme a tendency toward dictatorship, communities of interpretation are through and through democratic. As democratic they have evolved mechanisms for guiding semiosis and hermeneutics through open social institutions that keep the branching of interpretants alive and fresh. Pragmatically, all forms of semiosis must "earn their keep" in a competitive evolutionary semiosphere that doesn't have room for endless drift and sheer waste. The imagination, whether transcendental in Kant's sense, or ontic/psychological, feeds off of and then dispenses novel signs that can enrich and expand awareness of the more elusive orders 'within' *nature natured*.

The hermeneutics of suspicion looks at each sign series from the standpoint of its origin in a system of power that posits and guards the series from critique or query. Once the hidden power dynamic is exposed the relevant sign series is stripped of its governing power to shape and manage vision and ideation—the hermeneutic map is wiped clean, at least partly insofar as the sign series still retains some of its inertial charge. When several interpreters work together on destructuring the relevant semiotic order they in turn prepare for a reconstruction that works with fresh interpretants that emerge from a better use of method. Natural communities don't really have a method of semiotic analysis. They simply reiterate the stories of their signs and interpretants along power tracks that do not change—query does not exist nor do signs get examined once they are in play in giving shape to the meaning horizon of the static community. Communities of interpretation, by contrast, use some form of ordinal phenomenology, by whatever name, to explore and articulate the objects, signs, and interpretants of the innumerable orders of *nature natured*, especially those most pertinent to communal existence.

Communication flourishes in communities of interpretation as each interpreter enriches communal life by articulating and describing novel traits of the world. Of course, such communication need not always be, indeed cannot always be, of novel items, as genuine novelty is rare in nature. But communication can convey a new way of looking at the perennial, the stable, and pervasive—a way of appreciating their sheer prevalence, their power of endurance. In fact, interpreters can experience the wonder that anything prevails at all, that there is sheer prevalence, sheer thereness.

What kind of relationship does a community of interpretation have to time vis-à-vis a natural community? It has been argued that both types of community can be eschatological but in different ways, one pathological and one healthy. In analyzing this difference we will start shifting from the semiotic to the psychoanalytic account of community life and in doing so lay the groundwork for the analysis of religious life.

A natural community will control its members by a number of strategies but one of the most powerful is to control the future by envisioning a final end to history in a secular or religious eschaton that promises to overcome all of the tragic splits and diremptions of history. The community itself is seen as the special locus of history wherein its members have been chosen to be the vanguard, or perhaps the only members, of the consummation of life on this earth. In a secular eschaton, such as a communist utopia, history itself is seen as a kind of metaphysical ultimate that has intention and a conscious goal-like behavior. There is a telos built-into the march of time. In a religious eschaton the earth itself may be burned away by the divine power that will violently eliminate all non-community members. In either form, sacred or secular, there will be strict rules for inclusion and exclusion in the community and the content of the new world will be tribal and spelled out in detail. Natural communities, when under stress, internal and/or external, often evolve eschatological visions in order to deepen their hold on their members by sharpening the requirements for membership; namely, one must be 'pure' and take the appropriate oath to be part of the natural community and participate in its utopian drama at the fulfillment or end of time. In this process, non-community members must be demonized in order to tighten the reigns around the members of the natural community. There is very little that can be done internally against the powers of a blinding vision of an eschatology that solidifies all signs and (flattened) interpretants into a totalizing worldview that demands obedience and crushes any tentative growth of a nascent community of interpreters.

In a natural community neither the past nor the future are redemptive in a true sense. Rather, the eschatological or apocalyptic vision of the future simply takes the unthought signs of the romanticized past and extends them into a near time line that promises the utopia that looks very much like the life world of the eulogized past—a past that never existed. The symbols of community are unexamined and are enforced and protected against any use of hermeneutics in general, let alone the hermeneutics of suspicion that would both deconstruct the symbols of origin and the symbols of expectation. In a community of interpretation the use of hermeneutics, thematically or otherwise, is taken for granted and it is not always realized how politically charged such open ended methods of interpretation are—they probe into the origin and inner dynamic of the use and meaning of signs and symbols regardless of how sanctified they may be to the natural community within which the community of interpretation finds itself. An open free space of and for interpretation is often short lived unless there is institutional support for it. Dewey placed great stress on the reconstruction of institutions for this very reason; namely, that they have the power that individuals do not have and can protect citizens (interpreters) against the forces of inertia and control. Social reconstruction lies at the heart of ongoing democratization of communal life—and, as noted, communities of interpretation are democratic in thought, word, and deed.

One mark of a demonic eschatology is that it has tribe-specific content. That is, the vision of the impending future is of a depth transformation of the inside group of members of the natural community whose ties are of "blood and soil." These ties of origin are blindly maintained trough the static myths of origin that have clear inclusion criteria, for example, no Jewish blood, or "my ancestors came over on the Mayflower." The fantasies and visions of the future are entwined around the fictive visions of the past and vindicate, for their believers, the divine right of the inner circle of the tribe and those on the periphery who are deemed worthy of inclusion in the new being to come. The eschaton is to be given to the righteous and chosen ones as promised, perhaps, in a sacred text, event, dream, or charismatic leader. In any case, the eschaton will be constituted by easily grasped tribe-specific symbols and narratives that, by definition, exclude the overwhelming majority of human beings.

When a community of interpreters opens itself to the future and forms an eschatological vision the result is starkly different. The first, and most important, thing is that the utopian vision has no tribal content, that is, it is not filled with self-serving symbols that would serve one natural community over another. Quite the contrary. The community of interpreters truly opens the future by standing into the *not-yet-being* that stands before it as an invitation to transformation but not as a specific blueprint of a particular natural community. The liberating power of the *not yet* is allowed to permeate the sign systems and mobile interpretants of the community of interpreters, loosening them up just enough so that they can admit future prospects into their contours, but the gift of the *not yet* is not that of a private or tribe-specific revelation. Ernst Bloch describes the centrality and power of the utopian function:

> Therefore: the *act-content* of hope is, as a consciously illuminated, knowingly elucidated content, the *positive utopian function*; the *historical content* of hope, first represented in ideas, encyclopaedically explored in real judgments, is *human culture referred to it concrete—utopian horizon.* . . . Without the utopian function, no spiritual surplus at all is explicable over and above what has been attained and thus exists, however full this surplus may be of appearance instead of pre-appearance. (Bloch 1959: 146, 150)

With the utopian function in place the community can use its genuine surplus energies for the emancipation of its members from the pseudo utopias that are generated by natural communities. Hope has a concrete and historically pertinent horizon that belongs to it and its aspirations. For Bloch this content is part of a "bursting front" wherein the *Novum* (the radically New) can appear within the time process—a concept akin to Tillich's notion of the *Kairos* (fulfilled time). So-called subjective forms of hope are in fact supported by the *not-yet conscious* within the potencies of nature. Hope is a gift of *nature naturing* as its potencies can dissolve the closures brought about by the anti-utopias of natural communities. Thus the depth dimension of the *not yet* is rooted in *nature naturing* and lives as an opening/clearing within the heart of the unconscious of nature. As we will see in the next chapter, the *not yet* is correlated to the phenomenon of *god-ing* in the religious sphere of the selving process.

The *not yet* is part of the "how" of *nature naturing*, part of the way in which the depth-dimension of nature injects itself into the orders of *nature natured*. From the dark and taciturn depths of the self-fissuring nature emerges a free-space for the futuring of human communities and their human sign-users. The pulsations of the open and content-free utopia of the *not yet* enter into the inner structures and rhythms of the community of interpreters, enabling these somewhat finite and fragile structures to remain strong in the face of the inertial force of the enveloping natural community. The *not yet* is an actual ontological potency that lives by holding a space open within which utopian transformations can occur for the community of interpreters. Note, however, that the *not yet* has no specific or tribal content to impose on the communal selving process. Each member of the community of interpreters enters into the potency of the *not yet* in his or her own way and in concert with each other a communal way is forged democratically. Rather than seeking tribal validation in a 'divine' or secular monochrome utopia, the members of a community of interpreters seek a realist utopia that is trans-tribal and open to individual variations as they emerge from their encounter with the always-opening potency of the *not-yet-being*.

The most pernicious form of eschatology is that of the apocalypse in which everything is rammed through an extremely dyadic system that has its psychological base in a deep sado-masochism that takes delight in the idea of a maximization of human suffering of those who don't fit into the exceedingly narrow definition of who is saved and who is not. One could easily dismiss this as a species of psychiatric disorder that can be treated with anti-psychotic medicine, which is indeed possible, were it not so prevalent in so many cultures and religions. It represents a social pathology that has deep roots in natural communities and which threatens our democratic structures as much as any other social pathology one could name. The apocalyptic mind is both closed and violent and projects its high level of violence onto a divine agent who carries out the vicious sadistic fantasies for the sheer delight of the true believer.

We have thus arrived at three concepts of the future vis-à-vis communal life. The first is a content-specific tribal eschatology, while the second is the post-tribal future of the *not-yet*, and the third is the hyper-tribal world of the apocalypse. With the third species we move into the orbit of ordinal psychoanalysis. For in apocalypticism we see the most extreme rejection of healthy personal and communal living, indeed we see the utter desolation of the selving process and the reduction of the self to a burned out husk that is blown hither and yon by the dark winds of a mass delusion that destroys all creative life.

The drastically reduced 'self' that lives under the aegis of the great apocalypse experiences its own travail in a kind of semi-delicious masochism that dovetails with the sadism that is gratified in envisioning the ways in which the divine being will torture the damned. So while one must go through some masochistic pleasure at the beginning as a subject of self-reproach and some self-loathing, that too is pleasurable from the standpoint of the eventual triumph of the tribe of which one is a member. And the even deeper sadistic delights awaiting the 'self' complement the initial masochistic joys of wallowing in sinful self-flagellation. The apocalyptic imagination, in its bizarre crudity, operates out of a simple system that perennially captures millions of members of natural communities and threatens to pollute healthier forms of personal and communal forms of interaction. By definition, apocalyptic communities are anti-democratic and have a lock-hold on how its symbols are/must be interpreted. Insofar as they have a hermeneutics it is a hermeneutics of authority, which is really no hermeneutics at all. $Bullot$

It should be clear that hermeneutics, what I have called "horizonal hermeneutics" (Corrington 1987a), can only exist within a community of interpreters precisely because it requires open interpretive space within which to listen to the rich echoes coming from surrounding interpretants. The *emancipatory* eschatology of an interpretive community keeps its integrity by letting the *not yet* loosen up and hold open its future signs and symbols. At no point does tribal content, driven by the will to power, intrude into the processes of communal semiosis. Whenever it threatens to do so, the hermeneutics of suspicion, the negating part of horizonal hermeneutics, uncovers the tribal content's demonic link to the powers that seek to destroy the fragile community of interpretation and absorb it back into the natural community. While the natural community may out power individual interpreters, they can get reinforcement from institutions that protect and preserve their interpretive life. This struggle is unending but great gains have been made and communal life has occasionally become more open to its interpretive depths, but there is no evidence that something like's Hegel's triumphalist eschatology has operated in the many histories that have prevailed in nature. Again, while there are many histories and no one History, there is only one nature. Hence "history" is the species of which nature is the genus, although strictly speaking 'nature' utterly transcends the genera. For this reason one cannot define nature, as any such definition requires that the object defined be located in a genus and also be presented with its specific difference. Clearly nature can't be so located and it can't be different *from* anything.

The emancipatory energies of the community of interpreters are nourished by liberal institutions and vast, if fragile, open-ended sign systems that have their rootedness in the *not yet*. For Tillich (1933) bourgeois autonomy rests on a notion of harmony within a largely democratic state. He harks back to Kant's concept of autonomy as the state within which the free self binds itself to the universal thus further freeing itself from arbitrary and unruly inner forces. By imposing the universal rule on my self I fulfill my duty as a rational being and I realize my full freedom only by doing so. The good will, the only thing in the universe that is good per se, emerges with rational autonomy and makes the true ethical life possible. For Kant, autonomy is the goal of the Enlightenment and is the culmination of the education of humanity.

However, Tillich sees a danger in the Kantian paradigm of autonomy. While it is an admirable state in itself, having freed the self from its "apron strings" of the past, it doesn't have the inner strength to withstand true heteronomous (alien and outside) forces that can move in and shake up and even damage autonomy. In other words, the autonomous self is vulnerable to the powers that come from outside of its harmonic and safe world. Bourgeois autonomy is fragile in its top down universality, its vision of social harmony based on the rule of law and duty. It assumes that the social world itself is fully conscious and functions according to known rational principles. Its biggest mistake is that it sanitizes the unconscious and acts as if there is no depth dimension to either psyche or nature. For the autonomous self, rational self-legislating reason is all that there is and all that there needs to be. The community of rational beings has no need of anything stronger than autonomous reason to govern itself and live the authentic life.

This denial of the 'powers' is the Achilles heel of autonomous communities. They are vulnerable at two junctures that are linked together at the "heal." First, by denying the social unconscious they drastically underestimate its powers in shaping personal and social existence. Second, by maintaining their belief in self-legislating reason they ignore the many ways in which 'autonomous' reason can be distorted by forceful sign systems that have it in their grip but do not seem to do so—maintaining the illusion of being in control of all ideation. Put bluntly, autonomous reason is not autonomous at all, it only appears to be. Heteronomy encircles it from above (ideology) and below (the various layers of the unconscious).

Tillich introduces a third term to augment those of "autonomy" and "heteronomy," that of "theonomy." In theonomy we get a kind of relationship between the self and its world(s) that is participatory, that is, the self is grasped by a true depth-dimension of nature and the world that can best be defined as religious, in senses to be spelled out more fully in the next chapter. Tillich states:

> Autonomy and heteronomy are rooted in theonomy, and each goes astray when their theonomous unity is broken. Theonomy does not mean acceptance of a divine law imposed on reason by a highest authority; it means autonomous reason united with its own depth. In a theonomous situation reason actualizes itself in obedience to its structural laws and in the power of its own inexhaustible ground. (Tillich 1951: 85)

This depth-relationship empowers the autonomous self to hold onto its autonomy, valuable in itself, but by rooting it in sacred energies that are part of the *way* of *nature naturing*. Autonomy becomes sure of its own powers when they are secured in their own theonomous depths. Theonomy does not change autonomy or negate its life of reason. Quite the contrary—it strengthens the power of reason in the life of the individual and the social orders within which the individual is embedded. Kantian autonomy is preserved but only by a kind of theonomous grace that undergirds it from below.

With a theonomous base the selving process can continue in its social trajectory. It must work to open out the social unconscious within its own being so as to utilize its powers and inner forms (archetypes) for the good of the (hopefully) emancipatory community. Were autonomy bereft of theonomy it couldn't withstand what would appear to it to be an assault by the unconscious on its sovereign self-consciousness. But with some degree of supporting theonomy the self can commence the task of slowly integrating unconscious content into its inner circle of reason. And this is a task that cannot be avoided. The psychoanalytic law is that unconscious material that is not integrated and woven into the life of the autonomous rational self will be expressed in unintegrated and dangerous ways. The degree of disruption may be minor or it may be serious and threatening to the peace if many are involved. Social pathology has cost and will continue to cost millions of lives because heteronomous shadow material has not been integrated into the personal and collective psyches of whole communities.

We can look at social pathology from two directions. The first is from the perspective of the natural community that never allowed for the rise of autonomy, while the second is from the perspective of an autonomous (interpretive) community that collapses back into its natural community because it didn't, in this case, have a theonomous base to protect itself against the heteronomy of the natural community. Our equation is simple: natural communities are heteronomous, that is, they impose an alien law onto their citizens, while communities of interpreters are autonomous and may or may not evolve to be theonomous. Should a community of interpreters become theonomous it would constitute what Tillich would call a form of religious socialism or perhaps a theonomous democracy.

A heteronomous natural community will practice many forms of ontological priority in which selected items in its ontology will be ranked on a cosmic scale that is directly mirrored in the rankings of the social orders. This much is obvious, but what is less obvious is just how pernicious ontological priority commitments are and how pervasive they are even among the 'little' things of communal existence. This is why the counter commitment to ontological *parity* is so important socially, politically, psychologically, and philosophically—it opens up the innumerable traits of nature to be seen with equal presence and weight on their own terms. And it also shows how difficult the spiritual practice of ontological parity is given that priority schemes permeate almost everything that we envision, do, contrive, or undergo. From top to bottom we are prioritizing beings.

It is important to note that the commitment to ontological parity does not lead to the elimination of distinctions of value or worth or of distinctions of rank. Such distinction can and must be made in any living community and in one's inner life. However these distinctions are made for ethical, social, political, and other reasons rather than for some kind of absolute metaphysical reasons. I can say that a painting by Van Gogh is of greater value than a painting by my cousin and this claim would be accepted as appropriate. I can argue that finding a cure for AIDS has a higher value than a cure for the common cold and most would find this a compelling position to maintain. Or, I can stipulate that soccer is a more beautiful game to watch than rugby and I could at least try and make a case for good or ill. Hierarchies of all kinds exist and often have strong evolutionary reasons behind them, but in no case are any of these hierarchies tied to ladders of being. In the ordinal scheme there is nothing analogous to the metaphysics of Aristotle/Aquinas that moves from bare matter/potentiality to form/actuality with the former pair being less real, therefore less valuable, than the latter pair, which turns out to be the really real—god as *actus purus*. Indeed, such a view leads to the *reductio ad absurdum* that reality could get less and less real and simply fade away at the edges.

Both the natural and the interpretive communities are vulnerable to the social pathology that comes out of the great powers of the collective unconscious. The natural community is blunt faced, monolithic, semiotically flattened, reiterative, encased in habit, hostile to all outside others, blindly eschatological, self-absorbed, a cauldron of violence ready to boil over, patriarchal, and at war against any rise of autonomy. The community of interpreters is fragile, open ended, hermeneutically sophisticated, eschatologically open, non-tribal, non-violent, rich in novel interpretants, not self-absorbed but other directed, pluralistic, and capable of compassion (*Mitleid* for Schopenhauer).

The process of internal enslavement is similar in both cases. A natural community has already concentrated its power in a person or group who or which shapes most forms of public semiosis for community members. Its institutions can be bent toward the will of the Führer and all traces of novelty or any unique manifestations of personal selving can be nipped in the bud. The process is more complex when visited upon an interpretive community because its members are conscious of the heteronomous dynamics of the surrounding natural community and have resources for challenging the impending foreclosure of meaning. But, as noted by Tillich, if the community of interpreters isn't rooted in the power that comes from theonomy, a power that infuses it with the courage of the great "NO," it is especially vulnerable to the counter-power that comes to it from the heteronomy of the natural community. Autonomy quickly crumbles under the assault of the monolithic juggernaut of the power obsessed natural community. The overturning of the community of interpreters represents one of the ongoing tragedies of human collective existence. For much of our lives we live in the eerily smooth functioning of natural communities. Yet the free spaces do appear again and again, in which we poke our heads above the dark semiotic waters and see the prospects of a richer interpretive existence on the other side of monolithic patriarchal codes.

One form that social pathology manifests itself in is what Wilhelm Reich called the "emotional plague." He developed this idea in his reflections of the rise and success of fascism in Germany and Italy in the 1930s and 1940s. Writing from his exile in America Reich argued that the emotional plague is like a virus that is transmitted from person to person although the exact means of transmission is in the unconscious rather than through a literal virus per se. The contagion is quite real however and it can spread like wildfire if the conditions are right. It is transmitted through the deep feeling tones in the unconscious as these relate to a blocking of genital energy in the individual. From Reich's perspective, as a drive theorist like Freud, but unlike Kohut, our normal healthy genital sexuality is blocked by the social super ego and this produces pressure and a consequent anxiety in the body and biological/electric system. This pressure could be relieved with sexual fulfillment and the level of anxiety would dramatically drop. However, the reigning elite does not want its citizens to have a healthy genital life, as they would be less tractable and controllable if they were sexually fulfilled and not bullied by the social super ego. Hence, the leaders tackle the sexual issue from the opposite direction.

With the Führer principle in place the natural community can focus its sexual dynamics on one individual who will shape the dynamics of genital fulfillment for all members of the community.

The equation of repression = anxiety will be well used by the leadership. The individual citizen experiences ambivalence over his or her strong sexual drives and, in the Oedipal situation of patriarchy, will feel tremendous guilt over the desire to act out the fantasy of sex with the contra-sexual parent. The greater the (partly unconscious) desire the greater the anxiety and repression. If sexual release is out of the question then sexual misery seems to be the only option for the sexually maturing self. This is precisely where the demonic logic of heteronomous sexual control comes in. The Führer or leaders promise to remove all of your anxiety if you cathect your sexual energies onto the Führer and/or Party. You, in essence, castrate yourself in order to solve the sexual dilemma of the lose/lose Oedipal complex. By translating that unusable sexual energy into a 'safe' political energy that reduces your personal anxiety you sexualize your social and political life by depersonalizing sex and cathecting it into energy usable by the ruling elite.

From a personal standpoint the tradeoff seems like a good bargain. After all, the anxiety that comes from the blocking of sexual energy by the super ego is painful both physically and psychologically. If the Oedipal desires are also blocked off and they are the only ones that are active at that stage, then there is a doubly painful situation. There are two roads that can be taken. The healthy road is that toward mature genital potency whereas the unhealthy road is toward the bargain made with the fascist state—the extreme form of a natural community. The first form is especially hard for the individual if the natural community is a strong one. Genital potency is hard enough to achieve in the best of circumstances but in a fascist state it is especially difficult as the pool of possible partners shrinks with each triumph of the state over its inner 'traitors.'

Fascism is so successful because it acts like a religion keeping the religious super ego alive and well and imposing it on the patriarchal family structure, which is ripe for it. Writing a new preface for *The Mass Psychology of Fascism* in 1942, while in exile in America, Reich states:

> Fascism is supposed to be a reversion to paganism and an archenemy of religion. Far from it—fascism is the supreme expression of religious mysticism. As such, it comes into being in a particular social form. Fascism countenances that religiosity that stems from sexual perversion, and transforms the masochistic character of the old patriarchal religion of suffering into a sadistic religion. In short, it transposes religion from the "other-worldliness" of the philosophy of suffering to the "this worldliness" of sadistic murder. (Reich 1942: 14–15)

The demonic genius of fascism is that it already has the key ingredients in place in the natural community and the patriarchal family as its instrument, where the Oedipal triangle is redirected to serve the state system.

Reich further details the link between the patriarchal family and its tools of suppression of healthy sexuality and what this means socially and politically. The children learn their attitudes toward authority from their neuroticized attitudes toward their emerging sexuality. For Reich:

> What this position of the father actually necessitates is the strictest sexual suppression of women and the children. While women develop a resigned attitude under lower middle-class influence—an attitude reinforced by repressed sexual rebellion—the sons, apart from a subservient attitude toward authority, develop a strong identification with the father, which forms the basis of the emotional identification with every kind of authority. (Reich 1942: 53–54)

And the father becomes the fixation that elides over to the Führer who guides and shapes what happens within the family unit. The link between identification and submission is clear psychoanalytically and forms the glue that holds the fascist family and the fascist state together. Full genital sexuality becomes almost impossible under these Oedipal conditions. And certainly nothing like Kohut's healthy narcissistic self can find its flowering in a fascist family/state. Or if it does so its future is precarious and uncertain.

The community of interpreters will have a healthy sexual pattern for its members insofar as it has broken free from patriarchy and its attendant Oedipal complex. As noted in the previous chapter, when the child develops a proper and healthy narcissism it does not get entangled in the Oedipal triangle nor does it get frozen at one of the erogenous zones. Its transition to full genital sexuality means that it is not prone to the layers of anxiety that befall those who can't shake free of the Oedipal conflict that holds them back from mature genital expressions of sexuality. The State, fascist or otherwise, has no hook with which to catch the sexually free psyche and it instinctively knows this. Consequently one of the first things it will do is to invent the great lie that the genitally potent are actually sexually deviant and a threat to the community. The emotional plague is not just an event, it is first of all a directed happening under the partial control of the genitally impotent, the fascist elite who act out their own lack of genital potency.

Both the community of interpreters and the natural community rest on top of the collective unconscious and the unconscious of nature—a fact that is not fully acknowledged by either form of social congress, although the interpretive community will be more open to the prospect of examining its unconscious depths if the conditions of theonomy are present. Natural communities are not dangerous per se, but only in their more extreme forms, forms that do appear with a surprising regularity in global history. Since unconsciousness is dangerous in itself, the ignorance or even abjection of the unconscious is cause for concern and re-

quires constant surveillance. When a natural community radicalizes its eschatology and demands semiotic conformity it pushes
the unconscious further away from the sphere of what could be
called "social consciousness," thus opening up the space for the
release of a blind explosion of the shadow. For Jung, the shadow
is that layer of the unconscious that contains repressed sexual and
aggressive drives and contents and is contrasted with the persona,
which is the face we present to the public. The fascist state
presents a persona of discipline, order, social welfare and caring,
progressivism, and well being for the nation/tribe. The more rigid
and insistent the persona, the more archaic and violent becomes
the shadow. Underneath the 'good' side of a fascist form of natural community is a death-dealing machine that devours all who
don't fit into the crude notions of tribal identity. The more bright-
ly shines the social persona, the more darkly the shadow does its
anti-human work.

In a community of interpreters, the persona is maintained
more openly, perhaps more playfully or ironically. In any case, it
is understood that one's persona is a finite projection of a partial
aspect of the full richness of the selving process. In distancing
oneself from the persona, to whatever degree, the individual already acknowledges that the selving process involves far more
than sinking into a public role with routinized behavior and ante-
cedently specified semiotic codes. Further, there is an awareness
that the unconscious exists and must be reckoned with up front if
the community is to be relatively free of demonic distortions.
Within the interpretive community there is a sense that the collective unconscious contains powers, the archetypes, that eclipse
the individual in power and that help is needed in navigating
around and with them. A natural community lives out the archetypes blindly and hence does not integrate them into its public
life—they pour out their force into the natural community with
little or no resistance.

We can augment Reich's important concept of genital potency with a concept of "existential potency," which is meant to highlight the ability of the self, within its selving process, to achieve a full immersion in the rhythms of interpretive life and to do so with an awareness of the potencies of nature. The maximum potential of existential potency is to be found in relationship to art and its expression of the sublime as shall be phenomenologically described in the final chapter, where the selving process, personal and social, reaches its fulfillment, its inner telos and Aristotelian excellence (*arête*). Note that aesthetic naturalism uses the concept of teleology with great care and quite sparingly. It rejects the idea that nature *an sich* has a telos or that our species has a purpose or meaning for being. Rather, the concept of purpose is strictly limited to the intra-human sphere where individuals and communities can create finite purposes as part of their life-plans. Teleology in this restricted sense is developmental, that is, self-adapting to changes in the social and/or natural environment.

Regardless, the whole community of interpreters and its institutions must tend these finite and self-reshaping purposes with care. Each individual should be able to generate and maintain a set of finite goals and purposes that are reasonably consistent with each other and that have some over all harmony with the basic value systems of the community. As noted, each individual houses more sign series than can ever be made fully conscious or can ever be made fully consistent with each other. Under normal conditions this is not an issue crying out for amelioration. However, a crisis may compel the individual to build a new semiotic configuration that at least makes the layers of semiosis somewhat commensurate with each other. The goal of wholeness allows for incomplete and partial solutions, whereas the goal of perfection places an impossible burden on the individual or social body. And, the quest for perfection only makes the danger of a shadow projection that much more likely as the self imposes an impossible ego ideal on itself, thus leading it to project its own feelings of inferiority onto the Other. History is replete with instances of the quest for purity and perfection turning into acts of violence against the 'impure' and 'imperfect.' One's "purity" always has to be paid for by someone else, the untouchables on the edges of community life.

But psychopathology is only part of the story. On the other side is the quest for a just and healthy society where citizens can work together to create social conditions that foster both genital and existential potency. In what follows, normative criteria will be unfolded that guide our ordinal psychoanalysis of community life. Here we see how the community of interpreters becomes an emancipatory community by digging deep down into its conditions of origin within the potencies of *nature naturing* and uses psychoanalytic material in its quest for the proper communal structures for maximizing the well being of the multi-form selving processes in its care.

Nature's unconscious is neither anti- nor pro-human. It simply prevails in the way that it prevails; namely, as the eternal self-fissuring between *nature naturing* and *nature natured*. We humans are unique in that we can see and understand this "natural difference" and experience the sheer awe that it inspires in us. As noted, *nature naturing* is here defined as: "nature perennially creating itself out of itself alone." The stress is on the endless fecundity and ongoingness of nature as it continues to pour itself out into the world that we inhabit. *Nature natured* is traditionally understood as the "creation," that is, the world as created by god. Here the sense is different. *Nature natured* is understood to be "innumerable natural complexes," with no highest or lowest complex. To combine the two dimensions of nature we say: nature is all that there is and the sacred is in and of nature, not separated from nature or part of some alleged supernatural domain. Nature was not created it has always been and always shall be.

In healthy communal life there is a twin awareness; namely, that nature is open ended and not a closed totality of orders, and an awareness that the community is open in the same way. Here William James's pluralism is a radical and appropriate model for the metaphysics of normative communal existence under the constraints of finitude. James argues that the universe is both One *and* many but in different respects:

> "The world is One," therefore, just so far as we experience it to be concatenated. One by as many definite conjunctions as appear. But then also *not* One by just as many definite *dis*junctions as we find. The oneness and the manyness of it thus obtain in respects in which it can be separately named. It is neither a universe pure and simple nor a multiverse pure and simple. And its various manners of being One suggest, for their accurate ascertainment, so many distinct programs of scientific work. (James 1907: 68–69)

James has a proto-ordinal metaphysics that holds that neither oneness nor manyness is primary in all respects. In some modes of analysis and phenomenological description it is appropriate to assume a form of oneness, whereas in other modes a form of manyness is called for. James reinforces his pluralism by calling for a diversity of programs (methods) for research, each tailored for its particular world. Strictly, ordinal metaphysics transcends the distinction between the one and the many but for rhetorical purposes it sometimes lends its weight to the side of the many when pluralism needs to be highlighted against an overemphasis on a monolithic One.

The community of interpreters embodies James's methodological and ontological pluralism in the ways it goes about rendering nature and history intelligible and useful for its members. While there is no absolute One governing the orders of *nature natured*, there are many ones operating throughout nature and ordinal phenomenology traces out these ones within their ordinal provenance. James's wonderful word "concatenated" well describes the way of plural orders and their ability to also generate or reveal the numerous ones within the world. These ones and the co-given manyies are the skeletal sets of communal life.

The ideal of communal life, in its ordinal framework, is to live in and through the rich sign systems that constitute its body, the flesh that fills out its ontological skeleton (ones and manyies). The emancipatory (interpretive) community lives in the draft opened up by the *not yet* and holds open this future for the return of the lost object that will come to rejoin it out of the future. For Kristeva, as noted, this is the material maternal that precedes all positioned sign systems and which haunts us as we leave the realm of the good breast for the great realms of personal and communal semiosis. It is here that philosophy goes beyond the task of phenomenological description and the project of ordinal psychoanalysis and takes on the role of prophetic witness. For in describing the emancipatory (interpretive) community philosophy is compelled to make the normative judgment that this type of community is the telos of all communal life. Note again that for aesthetic naturalism teleological language has to be used with great care and precision, especially in light of its rejection by the Neo-Darwinian Synthesis. But this use of teleology falls outside of that quarantine as it applies to human self-shaping under evolutionary conditions that allow for its emergence and that have room to foster these values. Normative values may also have evolutionary value in their own right insofar as they give the human community greater tools for more capacious forms of adaptation. It is my belief that the emancipatory (interpretive) community has just these tools for species betterment and for a more just relation to other species sharing our semiotic world.

3

GOD-ING AND INVOLUTION

In addition to the complexities of evolution, constituting descent with modification, adaptation, natural and sexual selection, and inheritance, there is another force at play in the drama of our species existence; namely, that of involution. This second force in no way contradicts the Neo-Darwinian synthesis nor does it have any relation to creationism or any argument from design or an appeal to teleology or acquired characteristics. It operates in such a way that it is consistent with evolutionary laws as they have come to be established in science and, differently, in metaphysics.

Our species has no special reason for being other than the simple fact that it was able to adapt to its proximate environmental conditions for a sustained period. Nor is there a guarantee that our species will continue to exist in the indefinite long run. It has been astonishingly adaptive but for a comparatively short period by evolutionary standards. And it currently has a number of maladaptive traits that were once adaptive in earlier times of scarcity and intense food and reproductive competition. The continued habits from Paleolithic era adaptations may ill serve us now.

Involution works in a very different way from evolution and exists only in a rare and seemingly sporadic fashion. If evolution marks the external fit between an organism and its macro/micro environments, involution works internally to open up spaces for semiotic growth within the individual organism, and sometimes, under the right conditions, the social self. The external organism has fitness criteria related to reproductive success that can be fairly easily plotted by evolutionary biologists. The inner work of involution is much harder to grasp by external empirical methods and requires a kind of *empathic* phenomenology that can ease its way into the pulses of consciousness that emerge when there is an involutionary moment for the organism under study. Ordinal phenomenology becomes empathic when it learns to empty itself even further and stretch its intuitions in such a way that they enter into the stretching that occurs in the moment when involution takes place. Phenomenology is itself stretched by involution and represents one of the ways that involution becomes known to itself.

Involution occurs in only a few species, primarily the hominid ones. It was operative in those of our ancestors who are now extinct and is operative in a number of animal species. The requirement for its presence is a minimal degree of semiotic complexity and at least the rudiments of consciousness. It is most affective where the organism has some form of self-consciousness. Involution is a potency within nature that works in tandem with evolution at the 'upper' end of the scale of life.

It can be best approached through a phenomenological description of its most complete manifestation, which is in that of the human selving process. We will focus on the individual self at first and then on the social process. Involution will at first appear as a religious process within the momentum of selving and will be described as such using the language that is appropriate for its appearance in that modality.

As the word "*involution*" itself suggests, there is a movement seeming to come *into* the world from elsewhere. Something is entering into a state of affairs that was bereft of that content or force before the ingression. The ingression seems to be almost from an alien universe as it enters into the selving process with a vector momentum that is unlike the other matter that ingresses into the self. From the perspective of the finite self-consciousness the ingression/involution is uncanny and distinctive. It is experienced as a kind of stretching of the boundaries of experience, a kind of opening and clearing around the edges of the regular/ regulated forms of semiosis. The moment of involution is felt to be a potency of an opening that has its source in something larger than human, something divine or religious. The ingression is felt to be of a true sacred power that opens out the evolutionary matrix to an opening and a clearing that creates a space for a different kind of adaptation for the organism. This 'higher' adaptational possibility is not in competition with 'normal' evolutionary adaptations but has to do with the possibilities of meaning for the attending human organism.

Involution is experienced as a radical break from antecedent and present experience in all of its evolutionary modes. It enters into the selving process like the wind of spirit to blow open a novel aspect of experience on the edges of awareness. This coming-into-the-self-from-beyond is instinctively felt to be extra-human, indeed, divine. Perhaps the best term for this process, as undergone, is "god-ing," where the emphasis is not on an actual divine being of some kind but on the activity of a natural energy or potency that enters into the selving process *as-if* from a deity. Involution is thus seen to be part of the *way* of the deity as 'it' enters into and modifies evolution. Note that the idea of god-ing does not suggest or entail that nature houses a divine being who/ that actively modifies evolution in a purposive way. As we shall see, involution occurs without any teleological plan or cosmic mind of its own.

The energy of involution, experienced as a form of god-ing that intersects with my selving process, helps provide me with a brief free space of non-instrumental semiosis in which I can open up novel prospects for more complex adaptations to my various environments, social and natural. On another level, god-ing as encountered, can create a zone within which I can more creatively encounter my various unconscious dimensions: (1) the unconscious of nature; (2) the collective unconscious; and (3) the personal unconscious. Involution provides energy that works against semiotic closure and in that sense can help with the many complex ongoing forms of adaptation that evolution requires.

The issue of where god-ing comes from is a key one and an aesthetic naturalist metaphysics must weigh in on what the "god" part of the equation means. For the average individual the sheer force of the seemingly fitful and rare energy of the involutionary moment must have a divine source and that source must obviously be god as nothing lesser could explain its uncanny majesty. So god-ing must be the way that god communicates god's plenitude and power to the finite sign using self. But this way of reading the 'source' of god-ing is not compelling. For the current perspective, god-ing is a natural gradient that contains a purely natural energy that is a potency within nature that intersects with the powers and potencies within the selving process by a trajectory that is neither self-conscious nor intentional. That is, the 'source' of god-ing is not *a* or *the* god, but a potency within nature itself that 'descends' into beings funded with mind and the appropriate amount and type of semiosis.

For Sri Aurobindo the analogue to what is here termed god-ing is the "descent of the over-mind" into the world of ordinary consciousness. This descent is only possible when the world of human selves has reached the evolutionary point where there are enough sophisticated moments of self-consciousness available to house the descending over-mind. This descent is the cutting edge of involution and reweaves the soul back into matter thus actually transforming and spiritualizing matter in the process. Hence, for

Sri Aurobindo our notion of god-ing would be the crowning moment of the involution of the human soul as it works with the life divine to transfigure the world into a realm of spirit/matter.

One need not go as far as Sri Aurobindo and assume a strong impending wedding of spirit and matter to appreciate the argument that the over-mind is descending into evolution as an involutionary goad to individual selves who are unusually sensitive to the energies of god-ing. The sheer power and beauty of the involutionary moment truly deserves the language of *god*-ing and the phenomenological data reflects the word choice even if the referent is not an actual deity. Involution is itself quickening its pace within human evolution and will continue to do so as the fully natural conditions continue to provide openings for it. Again it must be stressed that involution is a natural process of opening and clearing that has no plan or goal for 'itself.' It is a gradient that, like the Dao, flows where there are open spaces within which it can collect and flow. Paradoxically involution and god-ing are blind yet they enable *us* to see more capaciously.

How does the self experience god-ing? What is it about the strange processes of involution that mark god-ing, involution's way of being-for-us, as distinctive and 'divine' for the selving process? Why is god-ing seen *as* god-ing and not as a simple psychological event with an extra layer or fold of semiotic charge? The answers can only come from an empathic ordinal phenomenological description of god-ing as experienced by the finite sign using self. We will do so by an imaginary case study.

The subject is a middle age Euro-American on his first trip to Mother India. He had been a student of Indian religion and culture from his teenage years and felt deeply at home in the Hindu worldview, to such an extent that it had largely replaced his own Christian heritage. He believed in reincarnation and karma and grasped the distinction between Nirguna Brahman (god without traits) and Saguna Brahman (god with traits) such that lesser deities like Krishna, Shiva, and Vishnu were manifestations of the god beyond all gods (Tillich). His own religious cosmology was thus that of Advaita Vedanta (non-dualism), which meant that the world of illusion, *maya*, is part of the divine reality as well. He rejected Buddhism's doctrine of no self and affirmed the existence of Atman or divine Self.

As part of the tour of the ancient southern city of Madurai the group visited the great Temple of Meenakshi in the heart of the great metropolis—one of the most important Temples in all of India dating from the 1600s. Meenakshi is the "fish-eyed" goddess who is the consort of Shiva. The subject withdrew from the group and meditated in a small dark alcove on one of the inner walls of the Temple. The darkness, lit up by numerous small oil lamps, permeated by the glorious smell of sandalwood incense, and punctuated by the occasional clanging of bells and blasts of horns, enveloped him as he sat transfixed and focused in the midst of palpable and visceral spiritual energies and currents swirling in the Temple and its vast grounds. Everything else in his racing mind slowly fell away as the Temple and its potencies started to reshape his labile consciousness. He sensed that something was about to overtake him from beyond his everyday horizon of intra-worldly consciousness.

Suddenly he heard a voice that wasn't exactly a human voice that would have used recognizable words in sentences. It was more like a presence that was appearing to him almost telepathically. It 'said' that it was the Great Mother and that it was ready to heal all of his wounds that were inflicted on him during his journey in this physical incarnation. The message was clear and had no ambiguity about it. Put in engineering language—there was no noise in the signal, just signal. But, again, the signal was not spoken in human language yet it instantly translated into the English language by the subject's finite consciousness. The message also conveyed an image of a large warm maternal shape that was enveloping and encompassing—a warm presence that would protect the self from alien intrusions and heteronomous forces. The vision ended as quickly as it came but left a feeling of peace and wholeness that lasted several days. On a subsequent trip to Mother India the subject went to the same spot to meditate but did not receive another religious vision.

From the perspective inside the self the message of the Great Mother was felt to be clearly and unequivocally divine, to be the presence of the goddess speaking directly to the selving process without mediation or filters. The Great Mother was what she appeared to be, a force that opened and expanded the consciousness and self-consciousness of the attending self—a force that enabled a higher kind of spiritual adaptation to the larger spiritual environment. The meditating finite self strongly believed that the Great Mother was an independently existing metaphysical power and potency that was as eternal as nature itself, indeed, that the Great Mother was the inner heart of nature, the depth dimension of *nature naturing*, to use the language of aesthetic naturalism. It was an encounter with god-ing if we can encompass the gendered language in this example.

The subject believed that he had received a divine message that, in turn, lifted the veil of illusion so that he could see the Great Mother face to face, in what Hinduism calls "darshan," which is the moment when devotee and divinity look directly at each other and acknowledge their respective gazes. In Hinduism there is no sense that you must bow your head or look away when encountering deity. Quite the contrary. What is in fact called for is a direct and ecstatic gaze that lets the energy of the deity into your finite vessel so that you participate almost literally in the surplus divine energy. In a very real sense, Hinduism is an energy management system with the deities bringing their excess energies into intersection with their human followers. This is one of the purest expressions of god-ing in our species being.

God-ing energies are thus the opening power of involution in which the individual self is opened into larger adaptive prospects on the spiritual level, prospects that can accelerate spiritual evolution. Hence, god-ing, regardless of how the subject sees the ontology of the object pole (god), augments evolution through involution, which in turn helps with spiritual evolution. Again note that involution is not some kind of magical divine intervention into the Darwinian evolutionary world. It appears only in those rare cases when there is enough surplus energy and free semiotic space for a quickening of evolutionary possibilities on the *spiritual* level. Involution can be indirectly adaptive when the spiritual level arches backward as it were and affects more material conditions of the organism.

But this is not the whole story. We return to Sri Aurobindo's notion of the descent of the over-mind as it relates to the experience of god-ing and the event(s) of involution. Aesthetic naturalism rejects both meta-teleology, for nature as a whole, and panpsychism for the orders of *nature natured*. Otherwise the concept of the unconscious of nature would make no sense, as there would be no place totally bereft of some kind of awareness. To reject the unconscious is to run the very serious risk of falling prey to its operations within the human collective and personal psyches. Panpsychism has the appeal that it does because it sanitizes nature and renders it friendly to human aspiration and desire. And the link between panpsychism and meta-teleology has long had a deep appeal to philosophical speculation on the nature of nature.

Sri Aurobindo speaks about how Spirit loses itself in the domain of matter, what he calls the "Inconscient," and struggles to free itself in its own form of spiritual evolution and involution. The over-mind and, higher up, the super-mind, descend into the terrestrial sphere and quicken the process of the liberation of Spirit and higher modes of consciousness. The idea of perfection slumbers in the world:

> For we are given a world which is obscure, ignorant, material, imperfect, and our external conscious being is itself created by the energies, the pressure, the moulding operations of this vast mute obscurity, by physical birth, by environment, by a training through the impacts and shocks of life; and yet we are vaguely aware of something that is there in us or seeking to be, something other than what has been thus made, a Spirit self-existent, self-determining, pushing the nature towards the creation of an image of its own occult perfection or Idea of perfection. There is something that grows in us in answer to this demand, that strives to become the image of a divine Somewhat, and is impelled to labour at the world outside that has been given to it and to remake that too in a greater image, in the image of its own spiritual and mental and vital growth, to make our world into something created according to our own mind and self-conceiving spirit, something new, harmonious, perfect. (Sri Aurobindo 1940: 1058–1059)

The human process finds itself fully embedded in a dark and taciturn nature that surrounds it on all sides and that limits its prospects for self-transcendence. Sri Aurobindo's conception of Spirit is too idealistic to function well in the current (aesthetic naturalist) perspective yet his sense of the struggle of nascent illumination to free itself from the blind reiteration of material habit and sheer inertial drift, within human experiencing, is stark and compelling. The "divine Somewhat" appears to us as an image or power of god-ing and accelerates involution within the selving process. What Sri Aurobindo calls over-mind, or super-mind, as yet more divine, is here seen as a potency of *nature naturing* that intersects with the human process under certain rare conditions.

Sri Aurobindo's cosmology, vast and beautiful in execution, can be regrounded and rendered more compelling through an aesthetic naturalist translation that deflates some of its claims and renders a humbler version into ordinal terms. So, concepts like "over-mind," "super-mind," "gnostic being," and "ascent," will be translated into terms better reflecting potencies within the one nature that there is—that is, in terms that are naturalistic, not supernaturalistic.

Instead of talking of an over-mind that descends from a higher plane of consciousness down into our realm of finite consciousness to quicken and illuminate it with divine energy, we can speak of an infusion of free-floating energy within *nature naturing* that quickens consciousness in its own way. This energy is not that of some kind of higher mind or some super being that is conscious of itself, entering into the sphere of finitude in order to launch a specific plan for the 'redemption' of the world. Rather, it is like a pulsation or microburst of pure expanding energy that cracks encrusted semiotic shells and clears a space for the rapid unfolding of novel semiosis. There is no need for a transcendent super-mind or consciousness of all consciousnesses to bring about the transformation of the selving process, individual or social. Most selves have little or no room to experience these pulsations or microbursts because they are totally ensnared in practical and narcissistic tasks. However, the instrumental and self-encapsulated world can be broken into by these 'higher' energies under certain conditions and, again, this inbreaking is experienced as if it comes from a higher world, hence, as a form of god-ing.

The attending self-consciousness experiences the microburst as a shattering of its semiotic rigidity and as a loosening of its habits of transaction and interaction. Reich's armoring segments can be weakened and even dissolved through the encounter with the involutionary power of god-ing as expressed in the selving process. The very process of opening, the moment of entering into the clearing (Heidegger's *Lichtung*), has direct adaptive value insofar as it enhances the organism's adaptive strategies and choices, providing a larger horizon of vision and possibilities. Involutionary prospects have evolutionary ramifications.

Emerson talks of the Oversoul in a way that has family resemblances to Sri Aurobindo's descriptions of the over-mind. In both cases, something either supernatural, or *deeply* natural, surrounds the human soul should it but be wise enough to see it. The Oversoul is akin to the Hindu concept of Atman; namely, the universal human soul that is but an expression of the divine itself, Brahman. Emerson's transcendentalism is one of the purist antecedents of aesthetic naturalism and represents a high water mark in the history of religious self-consciousness. More importantly, his work and vision mark the beginning of the transition from religious self-consciousness to the sphere of aesthetic transformation. He has antecedents before him, such as Schleiermacher, but no one who makes the transit in such a deep and compelling way, especially with a style of writing and thinking that is among the most beautiful and compelling in the history of the English language. With Emerson, involution takes a major step forward.

He had a clear understanding of the natural difference between *nature naturing* and *nature natured* and was alive to the potencies that punctuate nature. His poetic soul vibrated to the pulsations of a nature that was ripe and pungent. His idealism was of a sturdy and prescient kind, never of the cotton candy or sugary variety. Nature had bite and force and one had best be prepared to follow its leadings, its endless emanations:

> The method of nature: who could ever analyze it? That rushing stream will not stop to be observed. We can never surprise nature in a corner; never find the end of a thread; never tell where to set the first stone. The bird hastens to lay her egg; the egg hastens to be a bird. The wholeness we admire in the order of the world is the result of infinite distribution. Its smoothness is the smoothness of the pitch of the cataract. Its permanence is a perpetual inchoation. Every natural fact is an emanation, and that from which it emanates is an emanation also, and from every emanation is a new emanation. If anything could stand still, it would be crushed and dissipated by

the torrent it resisted, and if it were a mind, would be crazed;
as insane persons are those who hold fast to one thought, and
do not flow with the course of nature. (Emerson 1841: 119)

This Neo-Platonic idealistic vision of endless emanations is con-
joined with a rough and ready realism that takes nature straight
and as is, rather than as a fairyland of dangling metaphors. As
Emerson's vision seasoned and matured he became more and
more aware of the dark underbelly of nature and of the demonic
traits slumbering there: "Providence has a wild, rough, incalcu-
lable road to its end, and it is no use to try to whitewash its huge,
mixed instrumentalities, or to dress up that terrific benefactor in a
clean shirt and white neckcloth of a student of divinity" (Emerson
1860: 946). His realism is of a higher order, especially because it
also housed a place for an immanent transcendence within nature.

The natural difference remained key for Emerson and served
to frame the rest of his aesthetic vision. His deep understanding
of *nature naturing* has set the benchmark for subsequent forms of
aesthetic naturalism:

> Let us not longer omit our homage to the Efficient Nature,
> *natura naturans*, the quick cause, before which all forms flee
> as the driven snows, itself secret, its works driven before it in
> flocks and multitudes, (as the ancients represented nature by
> Proteus, a shepherd), and in indescribable variety. It publishes
> itself in creatures, reaching from particles to spicula, through
> transformation on transformation to the highest symmetries,
> arriving at consummate results without a shock or a leap.
> (Emerson 1844: 546)

Like Schopenhauer's Will, Emerson's *natura naturans* "publishes
itself" (objectifies itself) into and as the orders and complexes of
nature natured. Emerson stresses the sheer dynamism of the process as a "quick cause," that is, one that drives its works before it
in a blinding variety of forms. Nothing stands still in Emerson's

vision of nature. Each emanation is already restless with its own *not yet*, its own hunger for self-othering, its own need for expansion and enhanced scope. Emerson's *nature naturing* is fecund, forceful, unrelenting, capacious, forward looking, and endlessly self-actualizing as an infinity of signs decodable by the poet, "the newborn bard of the Holy Spirit." For Emerson, again, like Schopenhauer, the artistic genius becomes the human locus of transcendence *within* nature through his or her works that hold-forth the depth dimension of nature through the media found in *nature natured*. Salvation has shifted from the religious sphere to the aesthetic.   *Genious & pathy?*

The sphere of the beautiful becomes the *summum bonum* and the artistic genius is 'chosen' by nature to render the orders of *nature natured* into contrivances that house and magnify the beautiful. For Emerson, human texts, like the Hebrew and Greek scriptures, assume secondary status in the face of wild organic nature. Yet the object choice alone does not make a work beautiful—it has to be reshaped in light of the whole of nature:

> Nothing is quite beautiful alone: nothing but is beautiful in the whole. A single object is only so far beautiful as it suggests this universal grace. The poet, the painter, the sculptor, the musician, the architect, seek each to concentrate this radiance of the world on one point, and each in his several work to satisfy the love of beauty which stimulates him to produce. Thus is Art, a nature passed through the alembic of man. Thus in art, does nature work through the will of a man filled with the beauty of her first works. (Emerson 1836: 18–19)

Note that aesthetic language has appropriated religious language in this passage. The concept of "grace" now pertains to the relationship between the individual object and the cosmic/natural whole in which that object finds its own beauty. Universal grace is not bestowed by a self-conscious and historically active deity but is a natural event that simply *happens* whenever and wherever beauty is brought into the world by the artist by an act of "Will." The full radiance of the world of *nature natured* is concentrated on one nodal point where the potencies of *nature naturing* can come to expression. Beauty is second only to the sublime as a gateway to the eternal play of *nature naturing* and *nature natured*.

Involution works through beauty to cloth the selving process with the richest possible textures, tones, motions, and shapes of nature. But nature need not be reshaped by the human process in order to manifest and be beautiful. The interactions between self and nature add another layer to the beautiful if only by intensifying what is already there. And there is restlessness in our semiotic systems as they too struggle to embody and manifest the beautiful in their robust forms of signification—especially in the actual infinite qua actualizing infinite.

The concept of the "spirit" has made its appearance in our analyses and it is time to make our analyses and phenomenological descriptions of 'it' more explicit. Few concepts within theology have been so hotly contested or creatively ramified and few have been asked to do so much heavy lifting conceptually and experientially. The case in philosophy is of course different where discussions about the spirit have been much rarer and more circumscribed, with Hegel being an important exception. Aesthetic naturalism firmly rejects Hegel's quasi-Christian triumphalism and monism and finds that the phenomenological data points toward a vast plurality of spirits rather than one over arching Holy Spirit.

In Christian theology it is common practice to distinguish between the immanent and the economic trinity. The former trinity is that which exists from eternity in itself, whereas the latter is the trinity as it works in and through the orders of nature and, above all, human history. Aesthetic naturalism remains silent regarding the immanent trinity, as its ontological status cannot be probed phenomenologically, that is, it is not a part of lived religious experience. The economic trinity is also too far removed from the pulsations of god-ing and represents a monolithic categorical structure that says far too much about History as a unified phenomenon with one clear-cut trajectory.

The phenomenological evidence points to the existence of plural spirits, toward energies that enter into the moments of creative interpretation and facilitate the birthing of new interpretants. Peirce relates the concept of spirit to that of the semiotic ground relation; namely, to the *respects* in which a sign refers to its object. On this model, a spirit is a finite pulsation that operates in the between, holding open an interpretive space for the hermeneutic agent to find richer and more compelling interpretants. A given spirit does not house a specific interpretation, that is, it is not itself an interpretant or sign, but serves to *enable* signs and interpretants to find their rightful place within a specific given sign relationship. Spirits ply the between, the places where signs are not yet in play, where there is a tremulous vibration of possibilities for semiosis. In theology great claims are made for the Spirit; namely, that it is a person, that it is conscious, that it is the Presence of Christ in History, that it is the cosmic interpreter, that it heals and inspires, and that it is part of the very Godhead itself. As such, Spirit is infinite and has no 'need' to splinter into small moments of itself so as to enhance finite acts of semiosis.

If, however, we follow the phenomenological evidence we see that there is a finite and context-specific spirit operative at each nexus where an interpreter and each sign or interpretant meet. Clearly, the ontology of these spirits is different from that of most other natural complexes, but not impossibly different. A given spirit announces itself through a kind of breath or semiotic wind that opens up a small clearing next to a sign and its object—the spirit lives in the between and also deepens the between. It pushes itself into the nexus where the interpreter is moving with his or her interpretation. When the spirit is listened to, it sets the local interpretants into a vibratory pattern in which they light up the object to which they are joined. The finite spirit is the spirit of interpretation, again, not providing *an* interpretation, but enriching the prospects *of* interpretation.

The spirit *an sich* is harder to define and describe although some traits can be isolated. A given spirit is: (1) a finite energy charge, (2) a vector force, (3) a vibratory resonator, (4) an enhancer of meanings, (5) an opening power, and (6) a denizen of the between, that is, of the space between a sign/interpretant and its object. No spirit is eternal nor does a spirit have any awareness that it is a spirit, or anything else for that matter. But without the constant comings and goings of the finite kingdoms of the spirits interpretation would be flattened and moribund—a deadened prospect of the no longer rather than the open and opening world of the *not yet*.

Like Plato's Eros spirits live in the great between—between signs and objects and between interpretants. The best way to characterize each spirit is that it is a finite goad to further interpretation. For the sign using self, each attempt to understand a sign series may or may not receive help from a spirit-interpreter. The difference phenomenologically is clear. Without the spirit-interpreter there is little or no maneuvering room for the act of interpretation, that is, the signs and interpretants are closing in too tightly for the self to get the needed distance for a hermeneutic portrayal. The meaning-horizon feels leaden and closed. The self feels a semiotic pressure that makes it circle around a static point over and over again—reiterating a closed set of interpretants that soon devolves down into no longer interpretable signs.

When the spirit-interpreter enters into this closed matrix everything begins to change. The attending self suddenly experiences a brightening of its semiotic horizon and a waxing of its hermeneutic prospects. The world almost literally becomes more radiant as nascent interpretants emerge from the ironbound

world of deadened signs. Semiotic wakefulness replaces the leth-
argy that befell the selving process. The spirit-interpreter deepens the creative free zone between the nascent interpretants so
that the hermeneutic process can have the space within which to
pursue an enriched semiosis. The same-amidst-the-same gives
way to the different within the unified, with neither unity nor
difference assuming priority in all respects.

Since the spirit-interpreter does not provide specific interpretations, the responsibility for our hermeneutic choices falls wholly
on the shoulders of each of us as finite sign using selves. The spirit
opens out our world and makes choices available to us but does
not pick from among them. That aspect belongs to us. The question arises: how do we know which choice is the better or best
choice? This question is especially acute when we are dealing
with the energies of god-ing as they impinge on the human process. Further, for involution to work its way into the selving process we need to know how to enhance the prospects for *spiritual*
adaptation as it might in turn affect evolutionary adaptation. And
these questions are asked in the context of an aesthetic naturalism
that advocates a fairly strong determinism vis-à-vis the human
process as it finds itself in a vast nature that eclipses it in power
and scope.

The partial answer to the question concerning the criteria for
making judicious choices from among the semiotic possibilities
held open by the spirit-interpreter at a particular nexus should
not be a surprise. For it is in a community of interpretation that
the spirit-interpreter can manifest itself most clearly and power-
fully. Note again that the spirit-interpreter is not some kind of
intersubjective being with a communal blueprint that somehow
lands in the lap of all community members. The spirit-interpreter
opens the community of interpreters to its genuine prospects but
'leaves' the community to pick and choose from among them.

Each member of the community of interpreters will have, as a member of this special *kind* of community, a 'personal' spirit-interpreter with which he or she is working on opening up semiotic material for judicious appraisal. In communication with other interpreters he or she will compare and contrast interpretants and meanings that have intersubjective value and staying power. In each act of ramified communication spirit speaks to spirit just as sign series speak to sign series. Initially, the spirit-interpreter opened out individual signs and interpretants for the solitary self. Then it opened out shared signs and interpretants between selves. Then it opened out semiotic convergences among selves, all the while protecting personal meanings. At each stage in this outward progression the spirit-interpreter fought against closure and the dangers of a will-to-power that would derail the hermeneutic process.

The community of interpreters protects itself from demonic sign series precisely by its affirmation of the supremacy of the spirit-interpreter that lives as its 'chosen' inner light and life. The individual member of the community often needs help against the forces of heteronomy that threaten personal and communal existence. The spirit-interpreter not only opens up semiosis, it also critiques deviant or demonic forms of semiotic closure and control. Insofar as an alien sign series, coming from its own or another natural community, tries to insert itself into the community of interpreters, the spirit-interpreter will quickly signal that closure and a form of semiotic death mark the sign series' inner being. It is as if the spirit-interpreter has a built-in heteronomy detector.

The individual interpreter living in a community of interpreters relies on the spirit of interpretation to help shape and contour its semiotic home and world. Interpretation is ubiquitous but not self-grounding. It must be remembered that for Peirce, as for aesthetic naturalism, signs are signs of something other than themselves; namely, of objects and interpretants. Signs dig deeply down into nature and the various histories that mark the travail of the human process on this planet. The chief function of semiosis is to unveil the regnant traits of *nature natured* and render these key traits available to individual and communal selves. More specialized forms of query and inquiry can decide, or leave open, what ontological niche a given natural complex belongs to. This is especially the case with our concept/experience of god-ing and its personal and communal dimensions.

We have described the personal dimension of the encounter of god-ing. It is now time to look at its social aspect. As noted, one can talk of god-ing with or without a specific ontological commitment to the object pole of the experience. That is, god-ing may be the actual way a deity manifests itself to a community, or, god-ing may be an energy gradient that only feels divine. Aesthetic naturalism, for a variety of reasons as will become clear later, accepts the latter argument, but one need not do so to follow the phenomenological description of the phenomenon as it gives itself. There are pathological and healing forms of god-ing, although the former might best be given another designation.

For a natural community god-ing is foundational for its authority structure. It is experienced as a monolithic power that secures the finite and anxious self against any and all forms of ambiguity and doubt. The feeling is one of a rigid structure of armoring in which all life energy (sexual and otherwise) is bent in the direction of the Führer principle. The encounter with god-ing is analogous to being lifted up and filled with unlimited power—of belonging to the most potent tribe in human history and with merging my identity with god's chosen ones. All of one's thoughts and actions are known and monitored by god and given the stamp of approval. The world is simple: One Land, one Führer, one Folk.

In far less extreme versions of natural community god-ing is experienced as a confirmation of my personal and social existence. The energy I receive from god-ing is neither revolutionary nor especially surprising. Put from the other direction, god-ing has less material to work with in a natural community, as there is limited free semiotic space for opening out the selves of the community. Nonetheless, there is some muted presence of god-ing. This can be felt, for example, when a social ceremony, such as a rite of passage into adulthood, takes on an extra fold of meaning that was not strictly predictable beforehand. It was witnessed as an eruption of divine energy and power that validated the rite but did not call forth any novel or creative hermeneutic reflection— hence, again, we see the flattening of interpretants in natural communities. Or we see the magical stories that accumulate around the rulers of the community, each tale being a manifestation of 'divine' god-ing within the natural community. The primary function of god being to sanction the rulership of the tribe by the Alpha figure.

In a community of interpreters the energies circling around god-ing do not coalesce around any one human figure or institution. Rather, they somehow distribute themselves more capaciously around institutions and individuals that/who have shown themselves to have emancipatory characters and democratic modes of interaction. It might jar on philosophical common sense to see something as un-thick and ontologically tenuous as god-ing as having something like human style democratic leanings, but this uneasiness should dissipate once the following phenomenological descriptions are made. God-ing has its own law like principles of operation and phenomenology can see them in action in individual and communal contexts.

Remember that god-ing is felt as a pulsation or microburst of energy that seems to come from a supernatural (or vagrantly natural) realm. It carries its own sense of evidential compulsion and can short-circuit normal epistemological testing procedures—at least at first. The question naturally arises: what happens to the energy of god-ing after the original impaction begins to slowly dissipate? Where does it go and who or what directs it? In the case of natural communities the answer has been given; namely, that the full impact of god-ing circles around and then pours into the individual and institutional power keepers of the community—there is no real competition or choice in the matter. For a community of interpreters the situation has an extra layer of complexity.

When a burst of god-ing enters into a community of interpreters in does not coalesce around any one figure precisely because there is no one hyper-energized figure to serve as an attractor for that energy. A Führer is a ready steady state attractor whereas the community of interpreters has no such figure to stand out as a radiating fount of energy. That being the case, the energies of god-ing spread out over the individuals in the community and impact distributively with less intensity in each case. It is a simple mathematical equation. God-ing is a fully natural event that has a phenomenologically measurable amount of 'divine' energy to distribute. It can either pour its intensity into a leader or spread it out into community members in a (roughly) democratic social order.

Within the community of interpreters there are mechanisms for directly dealing with god-ing energies. There is a kind of native theological talent within such a community that probes into the realms of the gods, goddesses, and the divine, however configured ontologically. If theology can be (partially) defined as the slaying of false gods, then the community of interpreters is a theologically active community. It gratefully wrestles, or plays, with the dispensations of god-ing as they may generate specific sacred configurations. The energy of god-ing intersects with both the conscious and the unconscious mind, having an effect on each. The unconscious is hard wired to convert high energy fields into equally charged symbols that contain and express archetypal realities and truths. Thus, the upshot of god-ing is not just that it brings energy into the community and its members; it also is the pathway by and through which archetypes are set alight in the personal and collective unconscious. The community of interpreters has the hermeneutic tools to probe into, and be probed by, the depths of the unconscious in its various layers and dimensions.

A given archetype, say, that of the Great Mother, acts as an attractor for signs and interpretants that are iconic with it. Following Peirce we say that any new sign or series that has some trait that looks like, is iconic with, that of the Great Mother, will attach itself to that archetype and become bound by it. As such, the new trait, say, an image of a woman in the patient's real waking life, will be colored from then on by the reigning archetype. This problematizes his relationship to that woman because he will always project the image of the Great Mother on to her thus covering over her real personal reality.

Natural communities live out their archetypal projections in a blind and unthinking manner. They abject the unconscious and cut off all prospects of creatively integrating unconscious material. As we have noted, this is an explosive situation ripe for violence and sadism. The Other gets clothed with shadow material and sooner or later may (or will) become the object of brutal attack—or, at least, some form of economic constraint and control. The community of interpreters recognizes the Other in its own midst, not to mention in other communities outside of itself. And the community of interpreters recognizes the most important Other of all; namely, the unconscious.

For Kristeva we are "strangers to ourselves" and our relationship to our own unconscious is emblematic for our relationship to all forms of the Other (Kristeva 1991). If we can begin the depth work with the unconscious, in its several modes, we can also begin the work of healing communal existence. It is precisely this work that reveals the power of involution, as allied with god-ing, to move us forward as evolutionary beings.

On one level, or in one dimension, involution works independently from evolution, while in another in can augment the processes of Darwinian evolution. Both dimensions will be described. As noted, involution is quite rare in nature and occurs only in beings funded with some degree of mind and a certain level of semiotic complexity—ideally self-reflexivity or self-consciousness is required. Involution functions to open out and enhance the semiotic reach and scope of the sign-using organism so that it is lifted up out of the immediate *Umwelt* or Lifeworld of semiotic interaction. Involution works by creating the great space of opening, the clearing within which signs can be more deeply seen and understood. For Sri Aurobindo, as we have seen, involution comes about when the over-mind makes its descent into matter in order to free the spirit that is slumbering in the great "Inconscient." For aesthetic naturalism involution happens when the fully natural energies of god-ing impact on the selving process, individual or social, and move that process into larger orders of interaction.

One way to tell if god-ing energies are holy or demonic is to apply the criterion of ontological parity. That is, does the impact of the god-ing microburst set up hierarchies of the more and less real (valuable) or does it reinforce the full reality of all community members? On the individual level, does god-ing elevate only one part of my being against the others or does it elevate equally all of the parts of my full reality? If the energies of god-ing affect all equally then it has aided in the process of involution, if not then it has served as a retrograde motion and actually thwarts the process of individual growth.

If evolution means descent with branching/divergence, then involution means ascent with internal convergence. Again, this notion of ascent should not be confused with Sri Aurobindo's more dramatic and idealistic one wherein he assumes that the cosmic process is a monistic one already underway on our planet with a guaranteed triumph in the proximate future. Nor should the concept of "convergence" be confused with Teilhard de Chardin's notion of the Omega Point; namely, the end point where spiritual evolution will consummate biological divergence with the post-biological Noosphere which is convergent. Both Sri Aurobindo and Teilhard go way beyond the phenomenological data, not to mention the reach of the ordinal perspective. Convergence does exist in involution but it is ordinally located and fragmented, not trans-ordinal and all victorious. Ascent does happen, and is happening as I write these words, but only within some orders and only in some respects. In short, the ordinal perspective deflates grandiose schemes that would paint human-all-too-human traits onto the vast canvases of *nature natured*.

In the various fields of involution, opened out through the pulsations of god-ing, the human process experiences an increase in its own energy flow and its mood of attunement shifts, if ever so slightly in some cases, toward the ecstatic, toward the feeling of self-transcendence in time and space. A renewed sense of internal unity fills the self; a sense of wholeness emerges even in the midst of the various swirling pressures of *nature natured*. This feeling of unity reaches down into the unconscious as well as the self befriends its own alien depths. Note that this 'friendship' is never an easy or fully comfortable one, especially as the unconscious is hidden behind a veil of ignorance that keeps its mysterious contents out of reach for the attending consciousness. But without this fitful and precarious friendship there is little hope for healthy dealings with the Others both within and without the community of interpreters. And, of course, a community of interpreters can attempt to bring its own or another natural community to an inner transformation so that it too may contain seeds of an interpretive community. A perfect example of this is how the civil rights movement in American history transformed the racist natural community into one that was at least partially interpretive. Emancipatory seeds were planted and many grew and continue to grow.

Involution is ascendant and convergent. It ascends toward a state of enriched semiotic complexity in which sign-users become open and permeable to each other as all community members become what Jaspers called "ciphers of transcendence." A cipher is a zero point, a kind of clearing within and through which the light of transcendence can shine. "Transcendence" here means the radiance of the Sublime, which will be the focus of the next chapter. The ascendance is in no way guaranteed, contra Sri Aurobindo, and emerges in fits and starts in the ongoing travail of involution and god-ing. Convergence emerges when sign-users feel the gentle pressure of semiosis toward the post-tribal realm of open semiosis wherein transparency and empathy will guide all forms of interpretation and semiosis. For Schopenhauer, empathy or compassion (*Mitleid*) is the foundation of ethics because it is the deeper ontological structure of relationality. That is to say that compassion/empathy literally opens you to the Will and it's suffering in the Other so that you respond instantly and fully to their suffering, which is an extension of your own. Compassion is the ontological glue in human relationships keeping selves attuned to each other without the necessity of a mediator.

Like everything else, involution has its own evolutionary pressures to deal with. Not all involutions are spiritually adaptive and some, perhaps many, have to be rejected by the self-in-process. It follows that god-ing energies may not always have adaptive advantages. Personal and social critique act like natural selection, paring down 'random variations' to a select few. But it is not quite so simple. A microburst of god-ing is not the same as a given random variation. The latter is a structure that may or may not help the organism better adapt to a specific environment—it is usually a simple yes or no equation. The god-ing microburst or pulsation is not like a physical trait such as beak size and shape on a bird. It is an energy that loosens up sheer energy *for* more flexible adaptation. But there may be cases where the microburst or pulsation loosens up the wrong material and thereby diminishes adaptive potential for the relevant organism or sign system. God-ing, and the involution that it serves, face their own selective pressures even if in very unique ways.

But involution also works *with* evolution in other respects. If evolution sets the physical parameters of existence within all *Umwelten* (and human Life worlds or Horizons), involution opens up prospects for what might be called *spiritual* horizons of meaning. A species-specific physical *Umwelt* (environment) is a closed system needing little by way of new semiotic nourishment. It envelops the organism as its only world and provides all of the semiotic material that it will ever need. The organism traffics in signs even though it has no understanding of the sign → object → interpretant correlation. All of its interactions are quick and sure with habit taking control of all intra-*Umwelt* behavior. There is no semiotic space for deliberation or interpretive musement (Peirce), only the ancient blind reiteration of the same sign systems over and over again generation after generation until extinction rings down the final curtain.

In beings funded with mind and especially some robust form of self-consciousness and internal semiosis, involution adds to its arsenal of tools of adaptation both physical and spiritual. An evolutionary physical mutation can add one specific adaptive trait to the organism, while an involutionary expansion of the inner world of semiosis, say, as coming from a microburst of useful god-ing energy, can open up several adaptive prospects. Random variation usually ends in disaster for the physical organism. But the opening potencies of involution add several arrows to your quiver, usable now or at a future date. In spiritual growth involution deposits its treasures into a conscious self that can stretch itself out across time and space and hold back an adaptation until the situation is ripe for it. This ability to delay an adaptive possibility makes involution such an effective potency in the larger evolutionary landscape. Involution cannot bypass selection pressures through some kind of magical supernatural form of evolution but it can do a great deal within the selection pressures that surround it not only by adding novel adaptive strategies to the mix but by keeping the evolutionary landscape open for spiritual forms of transformation that have real evolutionary effects and implications.

We could say that involution is an evolutionary product, emergent at the very latest stage of organic evolution on this planet. This is not to say that evolution 'created' involution as one of its 'tools' for advancing its own aims, but that the potencies of nature expanded in a purely natural way to include microbursts and pulsations that we can't help but experience as modes of god-ing. There is no dark and mysterious telos buried within nature that cunningly produced involution and god-ing. For aesthetic naturalism the only form of teleology that has validity is that of Peirce's developmental teleology, which operates within the human process and a few animal species. This form of teleology is self-adjusting to changing environmental variables and comes with no guaranties of success in either the short or long run. Yet without it there could be no human growth and evolutionary expansion.

Let us be more concrete. Suppose I am in a natural community but don't know that it is one or even that there is another kind of community—which goes with the semiotic closure of natural communities. One day I personally experience a microburst of god-ing energy that concresces around a symbol of emancipation from bondage. The burst or pulsation frees me from my usual tactic of cost benefit analysis in which I weigh all of my

personal and social choices in terms of their costs to me verses
their benefits to me and perhaps my immediate family. I have
been living in a fairly closed semiotic loop even though I am
oblivious to any notion of semiotic openness or hermeneutic freedom.

The energy of god-ing lifts me up and beyond my reiterated
and highly grooved patterns of semiosis into a free zone that
leaves me slightly stunned and dazed, as I have no template
through which to understand this level of semiotic transaction.
The experience is akin to that undergone by Plato's cave dweller
in Book Seven of the *Republic,* who is compelled to come above
ground into the dazzling daylight and is deeply disoriented at
first. The initial feeling is a deep dis-ease and a desire to flee from
this demanding freedom and return to the tried and true habits of
life before the disruption of the god-ing energy intersected with
the self.   *God Analogy*

The first thing that happens to me is that I experience a break
between a sign and its object, that is, that signs are not the same
thing as objects and that there may even be an arbitrary correlation between signs and objects as reinforced by the community.
This discovered diremption between signs and objects opens up
the first awareness that there just might be other ways of linking
signs to their objects, other ways of creating new signs. It is an
easy step to go from the recognition that signs are more labile
than had been thought to the realization that there can be new
signs, that is, interpretants. For the first time I get the uneasy yet
exhilarating feeling that I can even realign signs and interpretants
in different ways and even expand my own self-consciousness by
seeking out other selves with different semiotic identities. The
entrance of god-ing energies has pried open the great semiotic
triad of sign → object → interpretant, which I now understand, in
whatever wordage. I can peer over the edges of my formerly
closed semiotic horizon and experience a moment of involution, a

quickening of hermeneutic possibilities. I have in essence become my own community of interpretation.

It is easy to understand the desire to name the source of the god-ing energy that made all of these changes possible. If nothing else, one wants to give thanks for the gift-ing that bore such amazing fruits. And it is built into the human process that it naturally converts energies into personified figures and forces. Thus it is highly unlikely that the average person would be content to talk about pulsations and microbursts rather than sing the praises of Krishna, Christ, Abraham, Mohammad, Buddha, and a host of other deities. Thinking generically rather than symbolically and pictorially is almost impossible even though philosophy has that as one of its goals. Perhaps the ultimate state of affairs would be to think about the object pole of god-ing mythologically but respectfully.

Whether I name the object pole or not, I am becoming more open to a larger horizon of possibilities than I had ever imagined possible. In fact, my own imagination is awakening for the first time as it now has the necessary free space within which to enter into a muted form of interpretive musement. My sense of self has already started to morph into a larger shape and has even begun to acknowledge the realm of unconscious signs—this is made possible by the god-ing energy that loosens up the rigid boundary separating the (abjected) unconscious from the attending consciousness. I have moved from a tightly bound self that has been shaped and controlled by the parameters of the natural community to a fledgling interpretive self that has begun to see through the massive distortions perpetrated by my natural community. The realms of semiosis, especially those of the actualizing infinite of sign series, have become available to me for the first time. But I remain shaky and uncertain in this new dazzling world, struggling with my desire to return to the "dreaming innocence" (Tillich) of my earlier life.

The inner telos of the selving process is to go beyond one's given configuration and become open to a more capacious horizon of meaning within the time process. Semiosis gets new energies for both intra and interworldly sign translation and the emerging new self lives in the *not yet* of openness. Leon Niemoczynski describes this sense of self-transcendence from the perspective of his own metaphysical perspective of "speculative naturalism," which has its roots in Schelling and Peirce:

> In transcendence one is seeking, as Schelling put it. "the world at large"-that is, one seeks to go "beyond:" beyond one's own particular world, one's own particular self, or one's own finitude. The "beyond" is an encompassing infinitude, but it is also transcendental, i.e., a sustaining infinitude; and so in either respect this "beyond," thus far understood as the divine's infinite nature is *supreme* or *ultimate* as compared to the finite. The supreme or ultimate nature of the divine cannot remain so far apart from finite thought, however, that is remains permanently apart from human perception, for it is generally recognized that the divine's supreme or ultimate nature makes it distinct from finite creatures and worthy of worship. (Niemoczynski 2011: 96)

The drama of self-transcendence is stretched between 'divine' energies and its own internal momenta of infinitizing. This process is akin to walking on a tightrope where on one side one can fall into an extreme psychic inflation that lets unmediated infinite content pour or even rage through finite consciousness, while on the other side one can fall into a sterile reiteration of what Hegel called the "bad infinite," that is, sheer magnitude without an infusion of spirit. There must be a careful balance between the realization of the otherness of the infinite and the non-inflated participation in the infinite.

The original impaction of god-ing energy only lasts for so long and the self must make its way after the energy disappears. For involution to continue other forces are necessary. This is one of the places where intersubjectivity comes into the selving process; namely, as providing the necessary power and force to protect the nascent selving energies that cry out for liberation and emancipation. I have been shaken and transformed by god-ing energies and now know that the community within which I live has demonic and destructive features and that there is another possibility available to me and those close to me, even if I haven't named it yet or fleshed out its contours.

As noted, I have been lifted free from the closed loop of deadened signs upon signs and have discovered the worlds of objects and interpretants. Spirit-interpreters have also come to my aid as I try on the tools of hermeneutics by way of probing into the astonishing wealth of new signs that I had no idea were there all along. Anger begins to overtake me as I realize how much of existence has been withheld from me and with how much of my own potential being was foreclosed right from the beginning. This anger turns into a critique of the natural community and, with the help of other emerging selves, turns into prophetic anger—the seeds of an emancipatory community are being sowed.

The emancipatory community is a type of interpretive community and can only exist within an interpretive community. It is manifest as the moment in which an interpretive community grapples with the unjust conditions of its host natural community, although sometimes it can act against an outside natural community through an empathic gesture of solidarity. For example, Americans got involved in the anti-apartheid movement even though the natural community against which they protested was in South Africa.

When I encounter another subjectivity that has discovered the same sense of injustice as I have, there is the prospect of forging an alliance that can put pressure on the natural community. My own shaky and tenuous relation to my *not yet* receives strength and encouragement through another person who now becomes part of the larger prospect of involution, that is, of ascent and convergence. This convergence of two selves quickly invites others to the cause and the positive inertial charge brings more selving energy to the quest for just conditions within the relevant natural community. An emancipatory community need not be large and indeed will always be dwarfed by its natural community both in scope and power. Its energy comes from emancipatory sources in the great *not yet* that lies within the potencies of *nature naturing*. Prophetic witness sends a strong signal to the natural community that its conditions of injustice have no warrant and that the current community stands under indictment by the emancipatory community. The issue of one of *both* power and interpretation, of justice and hermeneutics. Prophetic religions like Christianity and Judaism have great power to critique natural communities when the prophetic voice is encouraged and defended. At other times religions may serve to reinforce the powers that govern natural communities. Tillich contrasts religions that posit the powers of origin in gods of space with prophetic Judaism and its god of time:

> The myth of origin necessarily takes a *polytheistic* form. The basic structure of space as coexistence side by side drives all spatially bound existence into polytheistic mythology. . . . The limited origin is transformed into an unlimited one, without ceasing to be limited. And one's particular god becomes god of the whole world, without ceasing to be a particular god. But the contradiction goes further; the mythical consciousness creates all-embracing unities and tries to overcome polytheism by the *imperialism of one god*, that is, of *one* space. (Tillich 1933: 18–19)

So Wotan emerged in the 1930s in the German psyche as tied to the myths of origin of that tribe. As his mythic power grew and as the German sense of space literally expanded, Wotan hungered for world conquest; embodying the desire to devour any and all other gods of space and origin. But the prophetic god of Judaism rises up against such monstrosities: "It is the significance of *Jewish prophetism* to have fought explicitly against the myth of origin and the attachment to space and to have conquered them. On the basis of a powerful myth of origin, Jewish prophetism radicalized the social imperative to the point of freeing itself from the bond of origin" (Tillich 1933: 20). Thus the prophetic spirit operated within Judaism to conquer its own local and tribal gods of space and thereby became a universal principle of social critique for any society mired in its myths of origin. Prophetic time, that of the *Kairos*, brings the power of the *not yet* into the struggling emancipatory community. Hope is more than a human attitude, it is a gift of that *not yet* that has its roots in the heart of nature. As detailed in chapter 2, the liberating power of the *not yet* remains open and liberating as long as it is not concresced into a specific tribal utopia with tribe-specific content.

One final distinction needs to be sharpened; namely, that between the spirit(s) and god-ing. They both are responsible for increasing the flow of semiosis and enhancing personal and social life and for holding open space for involution, which they serve. How are they different? God-ing is experienced as coming to the self from a supernatural source and as having great intrinsic power. The spirit-interpreter is felt to be more immanent, to be more local as it were and not from a divine extra-natural agency—it doesn't come as a burst or as a pulsation. God-ing has a numinosity about it that makes it stand out from every other type of encounter, whereas the spirit-interpreter actually draws attention away from itself so that it can serve the rising of new and novel interpretants—it is not numinous. Metaphorically god-ing comes hot while the spirit-interpreter is more like room temperature. God-ing can shake up the archetypes and galvanize them into action, while the spirit-interpreter can help with the hermeneutic process of grappling with the now liberated archetypes so that they can present meaning in an assumable way by the finite attending consciousness. Finally, god-ing eludes prediction and comes and goes by its own laws, whereas the spirit-interpreter remains available on a more reliable basis, ready to open out that free interpretive space that makes selving, personal and communal, possible and actualized under the conditions laid down by evolution.

The travail of involution and god-ing is a dramatic and exciting one, operating on the edges of evolution while yet always embedded in the vast ocean of evolutionary possibilities and hardened actualities. Involution can't change the rules of evolution although it can modify and change the variables that go into the instantiation of those rules. Ascent and convergence bring new traits into the world, traits that are not just random variations. They are semiotic formulae that can open out new sign linkages and new sign prospects. The selving process is what it is because involution brings renewed energies to its unfoldings in nature and culture. God-ings punctuate selving giving it a boost of liberating energy that enables it to expand its meaning horizon in new post-tribal ways. Selving in both its personal and communal forms lives and moves within the rhythms of evolution and involution, honoring both while being especially invested in the involutionary advance that crowns the self with the richest treasures of meaning in time.

4

GENIUS, ART, AND THE SUBLIME

Geniuses create great art and non-geniuses assimilate what they create. This dialectic is as ancient as the species and is foundational for communal life. With poetic license one can say that nature uses the genius to create works that advance species interest but then often abandons the world-creator after the work has been forthcoming. The analogy to Hegel's world historical figure is apt if less grandiose. The correlation of genius and pathology, especially manic-depressive disorder, is well documented and reinforces the idea that genius has to be paid for by the host (Corrington 2003e). Were the host to do a cost/benefit analysis of the costs of genius verses its personal gains it is likely that the 'gift' would be turned down.

For Schopenhauer the genius is the tool of the Will as the Will struggles to find its objectification in the power and beauty of Platonic forms. We have noted that Schopenhauer's concept of the Will to Life is roughly equivalent to *nature naturing*, especially as applied to the depth dimension of the human process and its modality of selving. The self is the highest objectification of the Will in the known universe and brings the Will to its highest pitch of expression. In the phenomenon of genius, rare and of great value for species life, the Will curves back in on itself as it were to produce a fountainhead of potency that clarifies the nature of its eternal striving. For the average individual the Will to Life plays itself out along routinized pathways that merely reinstate the same of the same, but in the internal fire storm of genius the Will breaks open new pathways, new vistas. For Schopenhauer, a person of talent can hit the bull's eye, whereas a genius can hit a target that no one else can see.

With the creation of a work of art the genius has brought Platonic Forms into the world of space, time, and causality where they can be encountered by another subjectivity. Only the genius, on Schopenhauer's model, can wrestle with eternal Forms and capture them in the various media of artistic expression. He ranks the arts from the lowest, architecture, to the highest, music, but his particular preferences need not be compelling in an ordinal perspective, which would prefer to speak of the particular ways and respects in which a given art form is distinctive and unique. On his model music is the highest art because it expresses the Will itself rather than a cluster of Platonic Forms.

The encounter with art requires a special kind of consciousness that transcends our everyday instrumental forms of interacting with the environment. Following Kant who speaks of a kind of pleasure devoid of all interest, Schopenhauer describes a non-instrumental type of pure perceiving that can only happen through art:

> Suppose that the object has been removed to this extent from all relation to anything beyond it, the subject removed from all relation to will: then that of which one has taken cognizance is no longer the individual thing as such; rather, it is the *Idea*, eternal form, immediate objectivization of will on this level. And just by that fact, anyone caught up in this perception is at the same time no longer an individual—for the individual has lost itself precisely in this perception—but is *pure*, will-less, painless, timeless, *subject of cognition*. (Schopenhauer 1819: 222)

This pure perception, while occurring within the world of space, time, and causality, also lifts us out of the hustle and bustle of instrumental uses of reason and the edgy pressures of experience. The subject and the object elevate each other at the same instant. The work of art holds forth its Platonic Forms and makes them available to the attending consciousness, which in its place turns its back on the Will and lets the Forms caress it and momentarily lift it outside of the rush of temporality and the crush of space. The encounter with a genuine work of art, that is, one created by a genius, stops time and space, however briefly, from consuming their children. In that sense art and its assimilation is anti-entropic. In the "timeless" time of art one is freed from the pain and suffering of the Will to Life. And with the coming-into-presence of the Forms the basic architectonic of nature announces itself.

The genius has an unusually high degree of surplus "cognitive power" that is left over after instrumental needs are met. Through this he or she becomes "the clear mirror of the essence of the world." Unlike the scientist, the artist is not creating new knowledge but rather is bringing ancient knowledge/wisdom into its shining-forth in the work of art. The eternal Forms are the objectification of the Will to Life under the conditions of space, time, and causality, but they also point beyond these finite conditions. Thus the Forms occupy a unique position in Schopenhauer—they are in the world of finite interaction yet rooted in eternity on the 'other' side. The artist, in bringing these Forms into a finite work that stands into our world, also lives, however briefly, in infinity.

Schopenhauer describes the life journey of genius as one of intense struggle and travail in the face of powerful emotions. Unwittingly perhaps he gives a near perfect description of the correlation of genius and manic-depressive disorder:

> And it is well known that one rarely finds great genius paired with a predominance of rationality; rather, individuals of genius are to the contrary frequently subject to intense emotions

and irrational passions. The ground for this is nonetheless, not weakness of reason, but on the one hand unusual energy on the part of that whole phenomenon of will that is the individual of genius and that expresses itself through the intensity of all his acts of will, on the other hand a predominance of perceptual cognizance through the senses and understanding over that which is abstract, thus a decisive orientation toward the perceptual, the supreme energy of whose impression so far outshines colorless concepts for such individuals that their actions are no longer directed by the latter but by the former, making them thereby precisely irrational; by this fact, present impressions have a powerful effect on them, pull them in the direction of the unreflective, of emotions, of passions. (Schopenhauer 1819: 234)

The intensity of impressions draws the genius into a restless struggle with the so-called irrational orders of the world. For the restless manic-depressive there is always the strong lure of the next order, the next essence, the next Form, the next passion, that keeps the psyche always on maximal alert—the bow is pulled taught and ready to let fly at any moment. The world is filled with countless allures and one can never be fully satisfied with any creative product that is produced. For the manic-depressive genius the creative process is ongoing and never rests, even after the production of a consummate work—perhaps especially after such a creation. Yet within this deep restlessness there are moments of repose, islands of peace wherein one can let the eternal truths of nature sooth and heal the wounds of the world, in the orders of *nature natured*.

For Kant, genius is inborn and is a tool that is used by nature to enhance our grasp of beauty in nature. The genius makes exemplary products but may not know how they are created or where the ideas for it came from. Without the genius there would be no beauty in the domain of art:

> **Genius** is the talent (natural gift) that gives the rule to art.
> Since the talent, as an inborn productive faculty of the artist,
> itself belongs to nature, this could be expressed thus: **Genius**
> is the inborn predisposition of the mind (*ingenium*) **through**
> **which** nature gives the rule to art. . . . Yet since without a
> preceding rule a product can never be called art, nature in the
> subject (and by means of the disposition of its faculties) must
> give the rule to art, i.e., beautiful art is possible only as a
> product of genius. (Kant 1793: 186)

Akin to Peirce's theory of abduction, which applies a rule to case
in order to grasp the case through a kind of pragmatic a priori,
Kant's formulation stresses the telos of nature to produce beauty
through the genius who is the chosen agency for the application
of the rule—the rule being the harmonic intensity of form that
enshrines beauty in a finite work of art. For Kant, there is a
genuine form of teleology in the correlation of nature and genius.

Inverting Kierkegaard we can say that the genius is the highest
kind of human being not the Apostle or saint. But this also inverts
Schopenhauer for whom the saint brings a lasting kind of peace
that is unknown to the artistic genius. In our rethinking of the
role of art and self-within-community we will address this problematic and find room for both emblematic forms of life, the sage
and artist. The final point of comparison will be with how they
deal with the primary phenomenon of the sublime.

Leaving this discussion for the time being we need to raise the
larger question of the social role of art and its relation to the
selving process. Does art have a quasi-religious role to play in
shaping communal values or is it a potential replacement for religion? Is art an expression of its culture or is it, or should it be, a
rejection of its culture? On the individual level is the artist a
model for a non-neurotic self or is the artist fundamentally neurotic? How does art relate to ethics, both personal and social, or is
such a question inappropriate to the subject matter? Finally, can

art have place in the *not yet* that lives in emancipatory communities?

We will examine the communal roles of art and then look at the (ordinal) psychoanalytic dimensions as they pertain to the momentum of selving within community. Schopenhauer's reflections provide little guidance on the social aspects of art being primarily concerned with its creation and assimilation by the individual. The paradigmatic role of genius remains however. It is radically augmented by an analysis and description of emancipatory energies and powers within the community of interpreters that protects and preserves art across the generations.

It is important to state at the outset that there is no one role that art plays in the community of interpreters. Rather, it can play multiple roles as needed and called for. In the natural community art plays the role of a cultural commodity that has mere exchange value in the bourgeois order. Our concern is with its deeper roles in interpretive communities as they in turn put pressure on aesthetically moribund natural communities. The art of the *avant-garde* threatens the standing order of the natural community for which art must only serve to glorify the ruling elite—everything else is "degenerate" art.

Great art can have two simultaneous functions that appear to be incompatible but are not. On the one hand it can bring peace and joy to its assimilator, while on the other hand it can reject and critique the status quo, that is, be a great refusal. Schopenhauer understands the first function but sheds no light on the second. As a historical footnote, he received from Wagner a libretto of the *Ring* but failed to appreciate its revolutionary potential preferring the non-revolutionary music of Rossini (Cartwright 2010: 530-531).

For Herbert Marcuse art has a central role to play in human cultural and political evolution, opening up prospects of positive and realistic utopian energy. He is careful to distinguish art from so-called "political art," which he sees as a lower form of art and not as truly emancipatory. Great art represents a critique of both right and left wing pseudo-utopias. It speaks from out of the *not yet* rather than from a content-filled tribal eschaton, hence its true radicality. Marcuse privileges surrealism in a way that would have been anathema to Schopenhauer:

> Art is the imagery of the potential appearing in the established universe of existence. . . . Surrealism thus invokes an infinitely richer, denser universe, where people, things, nature are stripped of their false familiar appearance. It is an uncanny universe, for what could be more disturbing than to discover that we live under the law of another, unfamiliar, repressed causality; meta-physical, spiritual, but altogether of this world, not of some heaven or hell, a different order which interferes with the established one without abolishing it. (Marcuse 1972: cited in Marcuse 2007: 181)

A surrealist painting, say, one by Dali, not only juxtaposes novel and disjointed items, it also activates the unconscious, which contributes its own bizarre linkages to those of a stretched consciousness. The normal world of regulated space, time, and causality gives way to one in which all constant conjunctions (Hume) are deactivated and where associations are random and problematized. The underground world of surrealism usurps the world of bourgeois harmony and autonomy and disorients the perceiver. In this sense art serves to pry the participant away from the routines of everyday 'natural' perception thereby potentially opening up some small space for a critique of the signs of the community. The art of the *avant-garde* cracks open a free zone within the natural community.

But art also serves to reawaken the sensual, to liberate the repressed and bring it to expression. This "desublimation" is especially dangerous to the natural community as it represents an energy not under its control. Even Form itself is eroticized. For

Marcuse: "Thus art discovers and liberates the domain of sensuous Form, the pleasure of sensibility, as against the false, the formless and the ugly in perception which is repressive of the truth and power of sensibility, of the sensuous dimension as erotic dimension" (Marcuse 1967: cited in Marcuse 2007: 117). The genuine work of art, as working with sensuous material (Heidegger's *earth*), excites the living Eros of the perceiver and can loosen the armoring rings that get desublimated. The sheer beauty and power of heightened sensuality spills over the rigid semiotic sensual field of the "natural" self thereby shifting repressed and sublimated energies outward into larger fields of sensual engagement. Reich's notion of genital potency reappears here for in the engagement with the erotic dimension of art the individual frees libido for healthy sexuality, thereby saying "no" to the anti-Eros of the natural community.

The revolutionary aspect of art is seen in its open utopian participation in the *not yet*. We remember that the *not yet* is not a content-specific utopia serving tribal needs but a much deeper pulsation or opening within nature itself. Hope is a gift of the *not yet*, hence a gift of the potencies of *nature naturing*. In this sense, hope is a gift that comes *to* the self, not just a human attitude that one embraces by a free and autonomous choice. Hope is *gifted* to the self and its society. Art stands as one of the loci of this gift and is preeminent precisely insofar as it is less tribal than religious loci.

Religions are innately tribal whereas art struggles toward the universal, toward the depth-dimension of the human process. Religions have always functioned to create and sustain strong identity bonds within the community. From the standpoint of evolutionary psychology the nascent community, existing under conditions of scarcity in the Paleolithic era, needs to find ways of judging community loyalty for each individual. Altruism easily extends to kinship and to reciprocal forms but beyond that it becomes problematic. How do we know that a given person will be reliable in the search for food and loyal in times of external warfare? How can we trust the individual to share his or her goods and services with the community? In short, how can we trust the individual to always look out for the interest of the tribe?

The answer comes from religion. What is required is the idea of an oath that links the individual to the community in a public way. The oath ratchets up the commitment to another level in that it is done not only in front of all of the members of the community but also to the god or goddess of the tribe. The oath, unlike all other forms of utterance, is directly linked to the divine. This utterance cements the bond between the individual and the members of the tribe, living and dead. Tribal membership is now secured and permanent (Feierman 2009).

However, the logic of this membership doesn't stop with the solidifying oath. In order to truly belong to the tribe it is necessary to worship a deity that is tribe-specific, that is, a deity that is jealous of other deities. My oath is not only to tribe and deity; it is also to wage war with other tribes and their 'false' deities. Violence is hard wired into religious identity right from the beginning. My identity, intensified through the oath, can only maintain itself at this intense level through what could be called ongoing religious war. In this sense, all wars are religious wars, that is, wars that pit one tribal deity against another, one god of space and tribe against another god of space and tribe. This equation of religion and violence frames the problematic of art in an important way and we shall see if art represents an avenue to a new kind of human identity within and between and among communities.

Kant was fully aware of the logic of religious war and struggled valiantly to create a formal ethical system on a universal logical foundation that would undercut religious based ethics. Keeping religion within the bounds of reason alone meant removing its claws and taming its unruly passions. Kant was a staunch enemy

of pietism and any effort to enshrine religious feeling as a ground
of human behavior or an ethical system. His seeming rigidity and
sharp dualism between inclinations and duty represents his heroic
efforts to save humanity from being devoured by the heteronomous forces of religion. Autonomy, as the self-legislation of universality onto the self by the self must be protected at all costs.
Innate practical reason, in its pure form, if we may put it so,
protects the self from internal heteronomy (the unbridled inclinations) and external pressures (the unjust sovereign). At no point,
however, does Kant have a place for theonomy or grace, thereby,
so I would argue, undercutting the necessary depth-dimension of
autonomy that would give it real power over and against internal
and external heteronomy. In short, Kant underestimated the
powers of nature and simply had no place for the unruly unconscious either of the self or of nature.

Yet his critique of religion remains an important one insofar as
he demanded of any religion that it obey universal ethical principles that apply to any and all religions regardless of any supernatural revelations they may claim for themselves and their ethical
codes or systems. Abraham should not slay Isaac under any conditions, period. By reducing the ontological status of the objects of
religious discourse, that is, of god, freedom, and immortality,
Kant hoped to reign in the metaphysical fantasyland that had
protected religions from healthy critique and an informed skepti-
cism concerning its cherished objects. God can remain as an *as-if*,
that is, as a regulative ideal that can goad the individual toward
ethical behavior but this is only a stopgap measure until the individual becomes a true ethical agent acting out of duty alone rather
than out of fear of divine disfavor or hope of divine reward. When
the species of rational beings evolves through enlightened education it will no longer need religious props to govern and shape its
behavior—the good will will have replaced the evil will in all
rational beings.

Kant's enlightenment utopia may not be compelling as a realizable state of affairs but his formalism does shed light on the nature of the *ought* as it cuts across all empirical forms of ethical practice among the various human tribes. Insofar as religion stands in the way of the realization of the ethical ought, it must be critiqued. Yet the other side of the equation must not be cast aside; namely, the ways in which the religious impulse can be liberating and valuable for enhanced personal and communal life. But I intend to look at this side in a different way than is common. I intend to show that religion surpasses itself, and thereby becomes deeply ethical, when it sublates itself into the aesthetic. The telos, if you will, of religion is to become the liberating sphere of art and the aesthetic. This radicalizes Kant's project but has some of its warrant in Kant himself, as we shall see.

Peirce has his own ranking of the normative disciplines and makes aesthetics foundational for ethics on the grounds that aesthetics concerns the *summum bonum*, that which is admirable per se. It is given to perception in a direct way and provides the norm for all other realms of value. The current perspective (aesthetic naturalism) follows Peirce here and places aesthetics at the foundation of the normative disciples. Religion is harder to rank or to put into a hierarchy because of its sheer complexity and the ordinal perspective refuses to so rank it. It has deep connections with the aesthetic and the ethical yet can also be analyzed on its own and an ordinal account must honor these layers of analyses and phenomenological description.

The claim being made here is that religion is more directly tribal than is art. Religion serves to solidify and strengthen internal and external tribal identity so that each member of the religious group knows his or her place and role within the sacred canopy of the group. Religious art for the most part serves to crystallize this identity within a governing liturgical context that ritualizes the regular reiteration of the artwork. The chalice

presents and protects the blood of the founder and makes it rou-
tinely available to the communicant. The chalice at this point is
not, however, seen as an aesthetic object per se but as the place
where the sacred enters into the domain of space, time, and causality. That is to say that the religious artifact does not draw attention to itself as a work of art when it is functioning within its
religious horizon of meaning. Insofar as it *also* does so it opens up
a deeper layer within the religious that is properly termed the
aesthetic. In its full shining-forth the chalice is both religious, as
the carrier of the sacred myth, and aesthetic, as the locus of the
archetype of beauty under the conditions of finitude. This gives
the artifact a double potency, a dual layering of power and meaning that makes the object a sacred fold for the community of
worshipers.

For the most part, inertia and routine cover over the liturgical
object and keep it in relative semiotic closure. It is brought out
according to schedule and serves its function within the larger
liturgical order only to return to its enclosure during the rest of
the week or month—its radiance has been covered over. Yet this
radiance can return when the energies of god-ing enter into the
worship space and set fire to the object, letting both its religious/
mythological dimension and its deeper aesthetic/beautiful archetypal dimension spring forth for the worshiping community. God-
ing, as the pulsation or microburst from the heart of nature, elevates the special object into its religious and aesthetic fulfillment—its telos as it were. In what follows I will argue that the
inner telos of religious art is to become emancipated art *an sich*
and that religion itself, in all of its astonishing complexity, is
underway to its telos as the sphere of self-standing art that is open
to the sublime, a sublime that lives on the other side of all religious revelations with their limiting and limited tribal contents.
The encounter of art with the sublime will be the culminating
point of the selving process and of our involutionary journey.

The question usually arises at this point as to whether or not culture needs to be distinguished from nature, especially if one is going to talk about beauty and, more importantly, the sublime. Is beauty limited to human artifacts and the sublime confined to the immensity of nature? Or, can beauty be found mostly in nature but only derivately in human works that have aesthetic value? How does one separate culture from nature? We can make some preliminary definitions. Culture is that part of nature that has been in any way altered by human hands. It need not be honorific or grand, merely something manipulated in some way. Planting seeds or writing an opera both represent culture on this definition. Nature covers everything whatsoever including human culture or acculturation. The distinction between nature and culture is purely secondary and has some practical use but for a thoroughgoing naturalism, whatever is in whatever way it is, is part of the one nature that there is. An infinitesimal part of nature has been manipulated by humans and can be called the domain of culture and this domain has some clear and distinct traits that mark its uniqueness. Ordinal metaphysics does not ignore these differences, quite the contrary, but it does insist that all traits are natural traits, just differently natural. An aesthetics of nature thus embraces both acculturated nature and 'pure' nature, but in different ways and different respects.

Let us start with the phenomenon of beauty and explore its appearance in both nature and culture, remembering that the nature/cultural distinction is a pragmatic one that is not absolute but one that serves important purposes in a robust aesthetic theory. Phenomenologically several traits announce themselves rather directly as manifest in both a region of nature and a work of art. Following James Joyce, the phenomenal trait of radiance (*claritas*) assumes priority. In his *A Portrait of the Artist as a Young Man* he presents his own aesthetic theory as it partly derives from Aquinas:

But, temporal or spatial, the esthetic image is first luminously apprehended as selfbounded and selfcontained upon the immeasurable background of space and time which it is not. You apprehend it as *one thing*. You see it as one whole. You apprehend its wholeness. That is *integritas*. . . . Having first felt that it is *one* thing you feel now that it is a *thing*. You apprehend it as complex, multiple, divisible, separable, made up of parts, the result of its parts and their sum, harmonious. That is *consonantia*. . . . The radiance of which he [Aquinas] speaks is the scholastic *quidditas*, the *whatness* of a thing. This supreme quality is felt by the artist when the aesthetic image is first conceived in his imagination. The mind in that mysterious instant Shelling likened beautifully to a fading coal. The instant wherein that supreme quality of beauty, the clear radiance [claritas] of the aesthetic image, is apprehended luminously by the mind which has been arrested by its wholeness and fascinated by its harmony is the luminous silent stasis of esthetic pleasure, a spiritual state very like to that cardiac condition which the Italian physiologist Luigi Galvani, using a phrase almost as beautiful as Shelley's, called the enchantment of the heart. (Joyce 1916: 212–213)

The radiance of the phenomenon lifts it dramatically out of its normal sphere and lets its traits have a self-standing that separates it from the everyday. The "thing" is a dynamic unity of harmonious parts each contributing to the whole that makes for a beautiful object as it stands-forth into its radiance and clarity. Technically any object (natural complex) can be radiant although some are clearly more likely to. Why is this? Interestingly, Joyce argues that the artist can make any object in nature radiant regardless of its quotidian nature, but that is a special case. In our everyday trafficking with objects only a select few have any prospect of becoming radiant. Again, why are only some objects more likely to be the bearers of radiance while others are not?

The radiance of an object doesn't happen by chance. Other factors are at work. Following Schopenhauer we argue that forms or archetypes are crystallized and activated within the object radiating outward with their conjunction of power and meaning. Archetypes are intrinsically self-manifesting and alight on particular objects as necessary loci to do their work of binding the universal to the particular. When an archetype (or plural archetypes) ingresses into an aesthetic object it lifts it into a sphere of numinosity, that is, a place of radiance. Without the form or archetype the object would not have the distinctive kind of aesthetic radiance that makes it so compelling to the human process. So we already have two traits that are necessary conditions for the existence of beauty in an aesthetic object.

In addition to radiance and archetypes there must be what Tillich calls a "gestalt of grace," that is, there must be a higher order arrangement of the Forms of the work of art into a vibrating totality that is a harmony of contrasts. Process metaphysics has well described this notion in its metaphysics and it well serves our understanding of the nature of beauty. The work of art is the home for radiant archetypal formal patterns that house the vibratory dialectic of the harmony of contrasts. Beauty is what emerges from this rich field of struggle.

The experience of beauty is one that requires a disinterested consciousness, as noted by both Kant and Schopenhauer. For Kant, "One must not be in the least biased in favor of the existence of the thing, but must be entirely indifferent in this respect in order to play judge in matters of taste" (Kant 1793: 91). Instrumental reason steps outside of itself and lets go of its internal mechanism that lives in the kingdom of means. In awakening to beauty I quietly and quickly enter into a non-instrumental kind of awareness that almost literally stands outside of normal temporality. A work of art is beautiful insofar as it manifests the following traits: (1) a clear radiance that lifts it up out of the everyday phenomenal field of objects, (2) it embodies one or more self-manifesting archetypes, (3) its use of forms manifests a rich harmony of contrasts, (4) it activates the harmonizing tendencies in the unconscious, (5) it has clear boundaries and can be circumscribed by the finite appreciator, and (6) it is universal in scope.

The beauty in a work of art speaks to all aesthetic agents even if there may be genuine puzzlement at first encounter. This universality comes from the constellated archetypes that manifest themselves through the radiance. Further, the activation of the unconscious by the work is an activation of the personal *and* collective dimensions of the unconscious. The content of the work may be alien but with care and patience the depth-forms will grasp the assimilator of the aesthetic contrivance and its universal semiotic heart will be revealed. Unlike religious orders, aesthetic orders are not jealous of each other—they are surprisingly non-tribal or even deliberately anti-tribe. My preferences for one genre or artist are non-lethal and do not require me to demonize other choices or affiliations. Love of one manifestation of beauty does not conflict with a potential love for another manifestation. One can love Matisse and Chinese mountain paintings. One can love Wagner and Indian sitar music. The combinations, loves, and loyalties are endless.

The beauty found in culture is thus measurable and is bounded by the 'frame' of the work itself. Music has a beginning and an ending, paintings have frames, poems are finite, and so forth. With each genre there are boundaries within which beauty must appear. This finite locatedness makes beauty manageable and non-threatening to the selving process. Each encounter with beauty is a moment of direct participation in which the self is modified and remolded. The identity of the self is enriched and perhaps even altered by the radiant power of beauty. One could almost argue that the psyche has a built-in hunger for beauty, that is, a deep need for a gestalt of grace where its internal structures are brought into a harmonic convergence and then an expression in the outer world. In any case, the encounter with beauty in a work of art is one of the most satisfying experiences that humans can have.

Beauty is selective for the most part. The archetypes don't land just anywhere. In order for beauty to be manifest more fully the archetype 'behind' it needs to reside in an order that has a high degree of measure, harmony, symmetry, and balance—in short, the ingredients that classically and perennially go to make of beauty. Beauty seeks its own kind. Art follows this logic. However, art can also put creative pressure on this logic by evoking the un-beautiful as a means of protest against the canons of the beautiful. Yet, even here, the notion of the beautiful remains stable and fairly universal. Or art can make the 'ugly' beautiful through making it radiant and archetypal.

What about beauty in nature? If the artwork has its built-in boundary, what of nature that has no boundary? Can we say that nature per se is beautiful? Or can we say that only some aspects of nature are beautiful? For an ordinal perspective it makes no sense to say that nature 'itself' is beautiful, or that 'it' is anything else specific for that matter. Thus, there are many who choose to see nature as sacred or as god's body. But this way of thinking assumes that nature is a totality or an overarching unity that can be located and/or have one universal trait. Once this metaphysical claim is rejected it follows that beauty must be a trait within nature and hence ordinally located. Hence, beauty in nature must have boundaries analogous to the boundaries found in works of art.

Clearly humans have strong preferences concerning what is deemed beautiful in organic nature. Mountain landscapes, rocky seashores, great canyons, mighty rivers, vast plains, rolling seas, glaciers, and volcanoes top the list. We have a fascination for the dramatic and large, for the overwhelming and perhaps frightening. We are specially drawn to those places in nature that have not been altered by human hands or works. Extending beyond the planet we are fascinated by Kant's "starry heavens above," if not quite his "moral law within." For us, these are all places of great and enduring beauty, perhaps even of the sublime. Equally, however, we are drawn by the beauty in the small and the ephemeral, by the rapid zigzag flight of the humming bird or the dew on the morning grass. We habitually make selections, express strong aesthetic preferences and, when it comes to organic nature, more often than not converge in our tastes (Kantian aesthetic judgments).

For Plotinus beauty is built into the structure of the cosmos right from the start. From the first self-othering of the One, through the unfolding of Nous and the archetypes, to the descent of World Soul, on to particular souls, and finally on to matter, beauty shines forth in each dimension. In fact, love of beauty is one of the surest routes to salvation, partly because beauty is the one Form that is dramatically present in the dark world of matter in which our souls currently live and its appeal is direct and potent. Plotinus gives us a roadmap that is striking in its beauty in its own right and which serves to enrich and deepen aesthetic naturalism's understanding of the depth-rhythms of beauty and the sublime.

Nature, here in the extra-human sense, can indeed be the locus of the beautiful in specific orders and in specific respects. I can participate in the beauty of one given order of nature and marvel at its local and regional traits as they together generate and present a harmonic intensity that transcends ordinary experience. The gestalt of grace that unifies the traits, say, of a great waterfall, is created somewhere 'between' the subject and the object. That is to say that the beauty of the cataract is partly the result of my own shaping, but also partly the result of the specific natural traits that intrinsically call out for such shaping. The beauties of nature require the human assimilator to set them alight, yet they are already halfway there as eminently ignitable on their own terms. Much of non-human nature remains mute unless a great artist can find a way to reshape its traits in a novel way that finds some hidden beauty.

While it may take a genius to create beauty in a work of art, it does not take a special such agent to mediate an encounter with beauty in nature. In this sense nature is more democratic in its gifting of beauty to human assimilators. And it provides an endless supply of vistas to satisfy our deep cravings for beauty in our lives as aesthetic agents. The fecundity of beauty in nature should have also filled Kant with wonder. It is impossible to answer the question as to whether nature 'planned' to house the beautiful. That it does so does not make beauty supernatural in origin, but it does show that in its depths nature untouched by our species radiates its beauty in ways that transform the selving process and fills it with the unique kind of grace that only beauty can bring.

Thus far we have seen the link between genius and the creation of art and the beautiful. This was followed by an analysis of the special type of detached perception that correlates to aesthetic appreciation of the work of art. Following this we have seen the relationship between art and the community, especially the community of interpreters. Art was examined for its role vis-à-vis religion within emancipatory utopian communities and shown to be less prone to violence than religious based communities. The distinction between culture and nature has been drawn showing that it is largely pragmatic. Finally, six traits of beauty were described as they pertain to the phenomenon either in nature or in the work of art. In what follows we will start out by distinguishing between the beautiful and the sublime and then weave this distinction into the other categories and structures of the aesthetic naturalist perspectives. This will enable us to do an ordinal phenomenological description of the sublime in its various ordinal locations while also opening out the psychoanalysis of the correlation between the sublime and selving.

Schopenhauer is much clearer than Kant on the differences between beauty and the sublime as found in different subjective states. The beautiful is contemplated in the Platonic Forms that reside in works of art and in more tranquil scenes of nature. The sublime on the other hand is encountered when we see nature in its full life-threatening glory and our own significance shrinks to a small infinitesimal point:

> Then in the unshaken spectator of this scene, the two-fold character of his consciousness achieves its highest level of distinctness: he feels himself at the same time an individual, a fragile phenomenon of will that can be broken to bits by the slightest blow from those forces, helpless before mighty nature, dependent, prey to chance, a vanishing nothing in the face of monstrous powers, and yet at the same time the eternal, restful subject of cognition that, as the condition of all objects, is the bearer of precisely this entire world, with the frightful battle with nature only a presentation to it, it itself in restful apprehension of Ideas free and foreign to all willing and all needs. This is the full impression of the sublime. It is occasioned in this case by the sight of a power threatening the individual with annihilation, incomparably superior to him. (Schopenhauer 1819: 250)

Beauty is finite and clearly circumscribed whether in culture or nature and cannot threaten the self with annihilation or with a deadly assault on its being. The sublime, on the other hand, is experienced as an infinite given magnitude that can wash over and drown the individual self. Kant distinguishes between the mathematical and the dynamic sublime where the former is given in awe stuck contemplation—the. starry heavens above—while the latter is given in the raging forces of nature. Yet for Kant, the sublime is still a subjective state, not a property of nature. It is conditioned by consciousness not part of nature *an sich*. For Schopenhauer the sublime is trans-subjective, that is, it is a potency of the Will to Life that affects the will of the individual self as it contemplates the mighty forces of nature.

In spite of his subjectivizing of the ontological status of the sublime, Kant gives a wonderful description of it that is one of the most powerful and poetic passages in his *Third Critique*. It bears quoting in full:

> Bold, overhanging, as it were threatening cliffs, thunder clouds towering up into the heavens, bringing with them flashes of lightening and crashes of thunder, volcanoes with their all-destroying violence, hurricanes with the devastation they leave behind, the boundless ocean set into a rage, a lofty waterfall on a mighty river, etc., make our capacity to resist into an insignificant trifle in comparison with their power. But the sight of them only becomes all the more attractive the more fearful it is, as long as we find ourselves in safety, and we gladly call these objects sublime because they elevate the strength of our soul above its usual level, and allow us to discover within ourselves a capacity for resistance of quite another kind, which gives us the courage to measure ourselves against the apparent all-powerfulness of nature. (Kant 1793: 144–145)

Both Kant and Schopenhauer stress our littleness in the face of those forces of nature that we encounter as the sublime. And for both a kind of metaphysical courage is required to withstand the ferocity of nature. The aesthetic moment involves the still-point, where the finite meets the infinite, whereas in the encounter with beauty it is more like an encounter between the finite and the finite. For Kant the infinite is not a true infinity as consciousness cannot really encounter something trans-finite given its internal finite structures tied to the schematism and the transcendental imagination. Thus the sublime is experienced on the edges of the finite, not as something that actually transcends it. For Schopenhauer the infinite can be encountered *as* infinite because the finite self can experience the metaphysical Will through its body and since the sublime is infinite in its own way, the self can have a direct experience of it through a heightened bodily awareness filled with anxiety and vertigo. The dynamic sublime speaks from the Will that courses through the heart of nature and its potencies.

Shifting to different language we can speak of beauty and the sublime as they appear within humanly occupied *horizons*. Again we note the distinction between an animal *Umwelt* and a human horizon, where the former is a species-specific environment of transaction that is not self-reflexive and which consists of instincts and immediate sensations. While humans also have their own *Umwelt*, they also have horizons that operate in a different dimension which includes self-consciousness and at least a muted awareness, or a potential awareness, that the horizon exists *as* a horizon and hence as something that can be methodically probed and known. Further, our ancient *Umwelt* can also be probed and examined as it shapes our own instinctive and evolutionary trajectory through time. So, unlike other creatures we can open out our *Umwelt and* our horizons for circumspect analysis and phenomenological description.

In the encounter with the sublime we reach the extreme edges of our meaning horizons, through a kind of transfiguration that can take many forms. Jaspers privileges the idea of shipwreck wherein the self, in its depth-dimension of *Existenz*, breaks open to the Encompassing that lies beyond any and all horizons of meaning. We live in any number of horizons, some of which are reasonably available to us by introspection, while others may be buried deeply within the unconscious yet still have effects on the self in process. A given horizon is a field of signs and experiences that holds the self out into the world in horizon-specific ways. Thus one can occupy the horizon of one's profession or the horizon of a faith community, or the horizon of a political affiliation. In each case the horizon will contain signs and interpretants that are specific and sometimes unique to itself. A given self will occupy more horizons than it will be fully aware of and often the sign systems of one will collide with another. Part of the burden of the moral life consists of attuning these various semiotic horizons to each other. Prior to this is the even more difficult task of becoming aware of just how many horizons one actually occupies.

The selving process must traffic with a living and mobile world of horizons and bring as much light as possible to at least the major ones that truly shape its trajectory. Once a relatively stable contour has been created by semiotic means of construction and ongoing reconstruction, then the self is in a position to explore the edges of its horizonal placement.

As finite the self can never hope to attain transparency for its varied horizons of meaning, but it certainly can get a sense of their overarching momentum and finite telos. The hermeneutic eye can see to the edge of a given horizon and under the right conditions come to know that the self is living *in* a horizon that could just as well be another one—there dawns on the self that there is something slightly arbitrary about its horizonal placement. Suddenly the horizon is no longer the same thing as the world. When horizon and world are separated from each other the self feels a vacuum that gives it a sense of vertigo, a sense that the rug has been pulled out from under its feet. However, the self has other horizons at its disposal and the next one can come to the rescue to fill in the gap left by the previous one when it lost its status as 'world.' This process can come to a halt with the new horizon = world equation thus giving the self back the peace it had lost, or the new horizon could also undo its link to 'the' world and propel the self back into an abyss of meaninglessness.

The loss of stable meaning that occurs when a given horizon proves to be finite and arbitrary is but a foretaste of what happens when all of one's horizons face the challenge that comes from the earthquake caused by an encounter with the sublime. Jaspers' notion of shipwreck works just as well here as does that of an earthquake to denote the event in which all horizons, all realms of meaning, all personal sign systems, and all glittering interpretants, spiral down a black hole and the world suddenly looms large and threatening—raw and overwhelming, without comfort or a safe harbor to moor one's craft against the storm raging around the self. The boundaries that one finds in beauty are washed away and the immensity of nature consumes all. Thus we have the classical account of the sublime.

But is this extreme version the only way in which the sublime is encountered or manifested? Can the sublime be found in human works of art and can it have some kind of finite infinity that keeps it more attuned to the sphere of the human? Is it closer to beauty than the traditional accounts would have it? Is the sublime hostile to the human process and its needs for meaning? Finally, can the sublime be manifest in and to a community or is it confined to specific gifted individuals like artistic geniuses?

Let's look again at what could happen at the edge of a meaning horizon when its occupant the self-in-process becomes aware that it is living in *a* horizon that suddenly shows itself to be a particular horizon and not the world itself. This shock could come from a microburst of god-ing or simply from the movement of some interpretants in a radical new direction in which their 'object' gets redefined in a way that it can't remain in the same meaning horizon—the horizon develops a kind of semiotic rupture or tear in it. In either case the horizon is now standing over and against the self as an intentional field of objects that have become disconnected from the self. The world also pulls away as its reality is no longer being rendered available by the horizon that has just lost its status as 'the' world. This dizzying condition makes it profoundly difficult to get one's hermeneutic bearings again without some help from one of the other horizons of the self coming to the rescue.

Where does the sense of the sublime come into this dialectic of horizons and the world that horizons serve? Does the self have to suffer total shipwreck of any and all horizons before it senses the sublime or can the sublime be reached when only one horizon has become deactivated as 'the' world? And if the latter is the case, what, phenomenologically does this horizonal foundering look like to the self-in-process?

The evidence points to the idea that with each horizonal collapse there is the potential for an experience of the sublime at that moment. The phenomenon of the detachment of the meaning horizon from the world it elucidated is experienced as a kind of shock of non-being. There is a feeling of foundering and destabilization that enters into the selving process right at the edge of awareness as the horizon suddenly gets lit up as a horizon, What once functioned smoothly and without drawing any attention itself, akin to Heidegger's equipment (ready-to-hand), now draws all attention to its phenomenality as it lifts off of the worldhood of the world. The horizon of meaning lets a small gap between itself and the fullness of worldhood emerge before the self-in-process. This gap, this new abyss between the subject's horizon and the worldhood of the world, starts to draw intense energy to itself and take on a third position between self and world. The gap is now the locus of a unique kind of energy, neither a sign system nor just reality *an sich,* but a vibrating potency that emerges in the new between, the between zone that has now grown 'larger' as the horizon and the world it once served pull further apart.

From the standpoint of the human process this new gap, this sudden abyss in which the horizon that once *was* its world, takes on an intense radiance and force that goes beyond that of intrahorizonal sign systems. This new form of the between is experienced as the sublime, as the powerful and shaking force that lights up the very concept of horizonality itself. This experience is totalizing and takes the form of a finite-to-infinite correlation rather than, like beauty, being of a finite-to-finite relationship. The sublime links the entirety of the horizon, as an actual infinite of semiosis, to the finite self that occupies that horizon. As such the sublime transforms the selving process down to its very roots.

It must be noted that the encounter with the sublime is not analogous to the religious experience of a revelation. The latter concept carries with it two components that are not found in the self/sublime conjunction. The first is that revelation entails a supernatural order, a violation of the principles of ordinal natural-ism, and the second is that revelation entails that there is a mes-sage with distinct semiotic and tribal content. The encounter with the sublime, in contrast, is fully within the one nature that there is and it is without specific semiotic content, that is, the sublime is not some kind of super order of information or some kind of divine mind that passes on metaphysical truths. The encounter with the sublime transforms the self by illuminating the edge of its horizon of meaning and lifts that edge from its attachment to the world.

From within the experience of the sublime it is as if one sees the power and potency of one's horizon for the first time, espe-cially as it lights up so much of the world of experience and ideation. Knowing now that it is *a* horizon makes its scope and richness that much more impressive. Let's say that it is a religious horizon that explains the origin and goal of my life in rich detail. It had never become thematic to me just what my belief horizon was, or perhaps even that I had one. When a crisis, or perhaps a creative moment of god-ing, shook my horizon and a crack opened between it and the world, I could suddenly see that I was living in a framework that was not identical to reality per se. As the horizon began to reveal itself more and more as my personal (and shared) horizon I could see just how much it had given me and how well it had done so. This in itself filled me with awe. I found myself suddenly vacillating between two strong feelings, that of awe over the richness and depth of my intra-horizonal religious semiosis and the beginnings of the sense of the sublime that the horizon also pointed to the full phenomenality of the worldhood of the world. The combination of these two feelings goes to make the experience of the sublime; namely, the sense of the finite/infinite of the now revealed horizon and the infinity of the worldhood of the world that lies just beyond my horizon.

The sense of the sublime lives just on the outer edge of each and all meaning horizons, curled up there as if it were waiting for the right conditions before transforming the 'owner' of the horizon to find that zone through a variety of avenues, running from shipwreck, to foundering, to a burst of god-ing, to a shock of non-being, to a rush of vagrant interpretants, to sheer creative play with semiotic possibilities, or to a kind of random chance. However the self arrives at the outer edge of its horizon(s), the experience of the sublime awaits it as one of the culminating moments of its species existence.

This logic applies to the extreme phenomenon wherein all of one's horizons collapse at the same time, although this might be a limit case as at least one meaning must be intact for there to be any kind of self at all. Suffice it to say, then, that the sublime will be manifest when several meaning horizons pry loose from their relationship to worldhood.

What healing potential does the experience of the sublime have? Can the self relearn to live once it has experienced the abyss between its horizon(s) and the world that horizons serve to render intelligible? Is the self after this experience "twice-born" in William James' sense, that is, more deeply attuned to the rhythms of the real? The answer should be clear. The self that has been shriven by an encounter with the sublime has seen the awesome power of what a humanly occupied horizon can do to render world and nature intelligible and livable, both personally and communally. Further, the self now recognizes that some key aspects of its own horizon are arbitrary thus making it sensitive to the differing prospects in other horizons and other horizonal choices, that is, it acknowledges the centrality of a healthy pluralism between and among horizonal variables. The pluralistic self understands the depth-mystery and power of the world and nature that cannot be captured by any human horizon nor by all of them in consort. Finally, the self comes to an awareness of the potencies of *nature naturing* as the ultimate origin of the sublime. The experience of the sublime does all of the things that religious experience has attempted to do but without the concomitant tribalism and fierce identity politics.

In their carefully drawn taxonomy of the sublime vis-à-vis religion, Chignell and Halteman trace the concept through the eighteenth century to the present with particular attention to the different theistic or non-theistic modes that it can take. While I am arguing for the separation of the concept of the sublime from that of religion, their description of the existential experience of the sublime is compelling, with modifications:

> The first stage remains that of bedazzlement, terror, and transfixedness, but there is also a second, distinct stage at which the subject's conceptual or linguistic faculties are felt to be transcended or surpassed: she has a vertiginous sense of encountering something whose salient features outstrip her intellectual grasp, and her mind is thus "raised" over or at least beyond its typical cognitive transactions with objects (this aspect of the experience is reflected in the German for "the sublime"—*das Erhabene*—literally, "the elevating"). The sense of outstripping or transcendence can persist well beyond the point at which the initial bedazzlement or fright has subsided. Finally, third, there is a more explicit epiphany—a eureka stage at which the subject's affections or beliefs are changed, existing states are in some way strengthened, or familiar commitments are transformed. (Costelloe 2012: 185)

Existentially, then, the self is arrested and transfixed on the spot where the sublime appears from within the travail of finite experience. This bedazzlement is overwhelming and disorienting as it spills over and encompasses the ordinary routine of subject object transactions. This overflow, this super plenitude comes from the depths of nature itself, contra Kant, and is the ontological cutting edge of the sublime *an sich*. The selving process is transfixed and pulled and pushed beyond its current configuration—the elevation that would not happen but for the sublime. The self is encompassed by its own higher and deeper self—higher insofar as it stretches toward the ultimate *not yet* and deeper as it activates the lost object.

Their third stage, that of the epiphany, is described differently in aesthetic naturalism, going against the religious focus of Chignell and Halteman. From their perspective, the consummation of the experience of the sublime takes place in the religious sphere rather than in the post-religious sphere of the aesthetic. While their ontology of the religious 'object' is phenomenologically subtle, it remains embedded in what one could call the pre-aesthetic sublime.

The encounter with the sublime can take place within nature, as almost all theories note, but it can also take place in an encounter with another person and with a work of art. The same logic applies. The following traits must be manifest: (1) the finite/infinite horizon must be pulled back from the world, (2) the feeling of awe must be experienced at the fact that a horizon *is* a horizon (bedazzlement), (3) the self learns that some of its horizonal signs and interpretants are arbitrary, (4) the self becomes open to other human choices in horizons (elevation), (5) the self comes to see the depth and mystery of nature in its naturing (epiphany) and (6) the phenomenon of worldhood stands out in its contrast with horizons.

A work of art thus can be the locus for both beauty and the sublime and one can experience both in a back and forth momentum that links the work to the finite and infinite in turn. A truly great work will be both beautiful in a finite-to-finite way and sublime in a finite-to-infinite way, each reinforcing the other. Insofar is it 'contains' the six noted traits of beauty it carries beauty into the world of human subjects, via the special kind of detached yet attentive consciousness of aesthetic appreciation, while insofar as it can pry a horizon loose from the world of the perceiver, through its novel presentation of interpretants, say, in surrealism, it manifests the sublime.

Circling back once again to ordinal psychoanalysis and the momentum of the selving process vis-à-vis the domain of art and the aesthetic, we see that the process of artistic contrivance is not limited to the making of publically available artifacts. Even more important is the phenomenon of making the self into an artistic project in its own right. That is to say, the self must come to see itself as an art work in the making and that the various arts as practiced by artists represent models for how the self should mold and shape its personality into an aesthetic whole that manifests beauty and, perchance the sublime.

One of the most important genuine masterpieces to come out of the psychoanalytic movement is Otto Rank's *Art and Artist: Creative Urge and Personality Development*, which was published in 1930 when he was forty-four. Earlier we had discussed his theory of the birth trauma as it relates to the origins of the selving process. In this later text he continues to affirm the importance of this primal trauma but he locates it now in the cosmic drama of the quest for individualization:

> The art-work, then, as we have seen from our inquiry into the nature of aesthetic pleasure, presents a unity, alike in its effect and in its creation, and this implies a spiritual unity between the artist and the recipient. Although certainly temporary and

symbolic only, this produces a satisfaction which suggests that it is more than a matter of passing identification of two individuals, that it is the potential *restoration* of a union with the Cosmos, which once existed and then was lost. The individual psychological root of this sense of unity I discovered (at the time of writing *The Trauma of Birth* 1924) in the prenatal condition, which the individual in his yearning for immortality strives to restore. Already, in that earliest stage of individualization, the child is not only factually one with the mother but, beyond all that, one with the world, with a Cosmos floating in mystic vapours in which present, past, and future are dissolved. The individual urge to restore this lost unity is (as I have formerly pointed out) an essential factor in the production of human cultural values. (Rank 1930: 113)

The birth trauma is not a simple psychological event that leaves traces of itself in dim memory. It is also an ontological event, even a structure of being. It embodies and is the transition from the world of the intelligible character outside of space, time, and causality, "a Cosmos floating in mystic vapours," to the world of three dimensions and strict causal sequences. Once thrust into the realms of space, time, and causality, the nascent self is driven by the power of patriarchal cultural semiotic forces to let go of its dreaming innocence—to become a sign master in the worlds of interpretants. Yet the haunting presence of the lost object won't go away and the self spends its best energies, conscious and unconscious, in seeking to return to the realm of the maternal object. The creation of art is perhaps the most potent of the myriad means the self has to quest for the no longer, which it hopes will appear in the great *not yet*.

Rank argues that art has played a more important role in our cultural evolution than has religion, specifically that the concept of a *soul* came to us through the arts and not through religion:

In this sense not only did the development of the soul begin with art, but the process of humanization of the soul com-

> pleted itself in art and not in religion. It was art, by its embodi-
> ment of man in lasting material, that finally gave him the cou-
> rage to reassume the soul which, because of the transitoriness
> of its bodily form, he had abstracted into an absolute idea of
> the soul . . . but it does seem certain that the development of
> art has always striven beyond religion, and that its highest indi-
> vidual achievements lie outside purely religious art, until in
> modern times it completely emancipates itself from that influ-
> ence and even takes its place. (Rank 1930: 16)

In the free play of art the artist can open out qualities of the self
that transcend instrumentalities and reawaken a sense of an im-
mortal soul. For Rank art gives us a sense of individual immortality whereas religion works collectively to give us a sense of collective immortality, that is, a strong group identity. Unlike the
neurotic who protects him or herself by withdrawing energy from
the world thereby limiting entanglements and who places an "ex-
cessive check" on their impulsive life, the productive artist uses
energy to transform and remake the world into an aesthetic phenomenon. For Nietzsche the world was only endurable *as* an
aesthetic phenomenon.   ⸺

The artist uses collective mythological histories to weave a personal and individualized myth of radical individuation but steers
clear of the public forms of collective life. The individuation process is hard and demanding and the artistic ego follows a rough
road toward a personal apotheosis. If the neurotic husbands all
psychic energy by avoiding conflict and prospects for horizonal
expansion, and the average person follows along with the herd,
the artist forges a larger than life personality that encounters both
beauty and the sublime, even if the latter is experienced somewhat rarely.

For Rank, the goal is to make the transition from the life of
making art to the art of making life. He has his own open utopian
expectation in a post-art-work *not yet* that will come when the
inner logic of the aesthetic envelops all forms of being human:

The new type of humanity will only become possible when we have passed beyond this psycho-therapeutic transitional stage, and must grow out of those artists themselves who have achieved a renunciant attitude towards artistic production. A man with creative power who can give up artistic production in favour of the formation of personality—since he can no longer use art as an expression of an already developed personality—will remould the self-creative type and will be able to put his creative impulse *directly* in the service of his own personality. (Rank 1930: 430)

The new artistic personality will manifest beauty insofar as it embodies the six traits listed above, but most particularly, radiance, a rich harmony of contrasts, and self-manifesting archetypes. The self as artist has a radiant personality that contains many strongly contrasting traits that collectively build up a rich contour of facets that produce a harmonic integrity. Shining through these aesthetic traits are the archetypes that give the personality historical and cosmic (natural) depth. When these are combined you have a "beautiful soul," but not in Hegel's more pejorative sense.

An artistic personality can also manifest the sublime when it lives out of the tension between a fractured horizon and the world that the horizon used to serve. This ontological wound reactivates the birth trauma and compels the self to search that much more frantically to find the lost mother. In the art works that emerge from this torn horizon the sense of the sublime will be present and the person of the artist will manifest this sublimity as well. Thus both work and creator manifest the sublime on the edges of artistic contrivance.

Rank rejects much of Freud's classical drive theory linking him indirectly to Kohut. For Rank it is the creative will that makes the self what it is, not the erogenous zones of the infant to which the neurotic is compelled to return. Rank's perspective is forward looking and affirmative of the essence of the human process. Like Kohut he sees the selving process as involving a healthy ego affirmation and a strong creative component that moves outward toward interworldly involvements. The artist has a "will-to-style" that imposes itself on the media of artistic contrivance, stamping the media with his or her unique other-directed personality. The artist, as a higher human type, no longer uses "the collective ideology of religion to perpetuate himself, but the personal religion of genius, which is the precondition of any productions by the individual artist-type" (Rank 1930: 45). The religion of genius is the true *Kunstreligion* as annunciated by German Romanticism and above all by Wagner with his notion of a "collective art work" (*Gesamtkunstwerk*).

Insofar as the artist type can replace the neurotic type the community can be the locus for an experience of the sublime. We have seen how the community of interpreters can become an emancipatory community when the conditions of justice become activated in the *not yet*. And we have seen, following Marcuse, how art can be both revolutionary and sensual, thus evoking its own *not yet* to and for the community of interpreters. Communities, just like individuals, need to have a sense of beauty operating within their meaning horizons. Artists function as the *avant-garde* for the interpretive community, shaking up hermeneutic routine and overturning habitual semiotic pathways of interaction. The creation of beautiful art works that house Platonic Forms has a direct social value in giving community members material for their personal selving processes. These 'private' encounters with beauty then become rewoven back into the communal sign systems and add the richness that comes from individuation.

The sense of the *social* sublime emerges when the community experiences a collective tear in its encompassing sign horizon. Suddenly the sheer grandeur of its overarching mythical universe is brought into focus as a distinct thematic object over and against it. The divorce between horizon and world opens up in the same way that it does for the individual but obviously with greater impact for the individuals involved. The loss of the reigning social horizon shakes the community to its roots. The sense of the sublime again emerges when the members of the community sense the finite-to-infinite dialectic that connects their finite mode of consciousness to the infinity of the horizon and its world now lost. This could be experienced during a period of profound political upheaval or of a major economic catastrophe, although less extreme events could also trigger the severance of the social horizon from its link to the world it had described and illuminated.

We have been arguing that the sublime is a reality in itself rather than a mere subjective state that befalls human consciousness when there are certain triggers in the environment. The ontological status of the sublime is partly unique in that it lives in the great between, that is, it lies between the subject and object poles of experience, opening each dimension or side to the other. On the one hand the sublime is not just bigness over and against our littleness, while on the other hand it is not just what causes us to be fearful as opposed to the quiet joy we experience when we encounter beauty. The sublime is certainly 'big' but in a special sense. It is big in the sense that it encompasses all horizons without being a horizon itself. For Jaspers the technical term for this reality is the Encompassing. The sublime can be called the Encompassing in this specific sense; namely, as that which can never *be* encompassed, but which encompasses any and all meaning horizons, both personal and communal.

For ordinal psychoanalysis the encounter with the sublime/encompassing reawakens the memory of the birth trauma, not literally but structurally. The lost object, Kristeva's "material maternal," continues to haunt the self-in-process as it works its way through the actual infinite of semiotic sign series in the public worlds of semiosis. As the inner powers of individuation take hold of the selving process, the lost object recedes from memory and becomes abjected by the patriarchal codes that constitute the "name of the Father," for Kristeva. But the material maternal is never totally lost. It speaks to the self through art and *avant-garde* thinking. Poetic language, speaking out of the ecstasy of *jouissance*, reignites the lost object making it partially available to the self. The return of the lost object is most fully achieved through all of the arts, even though Kristeva privileges poetry.

How do the two carriers of the sublime differ; namely, the saint or sage and the genius? We have noted the relationship between the genius and the creation of beauty in works of art. And we have noted Schopenhauer's notion that the saint stills the striving of the Will to Life permanently by a mighty act of using the Will to negate itself, thus transcending the artist who can only still the Will for brief moments at a time. Perhaps there is another way to think through this correlation of genius and saint, one that shows a deeper aspect to artistic production and its relation to the sublime.

Both the genius and the saint attain a different type of consciousness from that of most persons. It is a mode of consciousness that leaves behind the usual intraworldly modalities of finite space, time, and causality, while still, of course, being under their sway. This dual consciousness permeates everything that the genius and saint do, say, or enact. They are in the world in the same ways that the rest of their species members are yet also in the world differently, that is, they have a foot in another realm that is not strictly contiguous with this one. There is a breath of eternity about them, something of another world that makes them appear uncanny or alien to this world of quotidian concerns and problems.

Both the artist and the saint are fully aware of the duality of their lives, that they live in a public world that cannot, in principle, understand the other and deeper world that claims their true allegiance. They are split and know it. Part of the force of their lives is that they must struggle heroically to heal this split through the means available to their psychological type. For the artist it is, of course, through art works that are publically available for appraisal and assimilation. For the saint, on the other hand, it is through a kind of higher action that is actually a non-action, a kind of *Gelassenheit*, or mode of attunement that harmonizes the various components of the self into one higher harmony.

The genius is driven to make a product whereas the saint has no such compulsion seeing his or her life project as the 'product,' rather than the creation of some external artifact. The genius has a built-in restlessness because the product has as one of its goals the return of the material maternal under the conditions of time, space, and causality. That is, the given work of art is not simply an object with aesthetic traits; it is also a carrier of the unconscious link to the lost object. It reawakens the connection between the self and its pre-natal conditions of origin. The no longer gets called-forth from the *not yet,* which brings the lost object into the present via the route of the future. That is, the lost object comes to the self-in-process from the opening future that fills the present with its creative possibilities.

But the work of art, no matter how beautiful and fecund, can only do so much to restore the lost object under the constraints of finitude. The satisfaction it brings is indeed great and lasts far longer than Schopenhauer's model would indicate. There is a deep down primal satisfaction to the artistic life that goes beyond the joys of this or that work as produced. Yet there remains the gap between the work as done and the goad to fill in the gap between the broken horizon and the world through more work. For the manic-depressive genius even a relatively fulfilled existence remains driven to find the 'perfect' art work that will return the material maternal in all of its lost glory. The myth animating the life of the artist is that of Orpheus in the underworld where

his music was so beautiful and powerful that it stopped the wheel
of Ixion from its torturous spinning while he was playing.

The genius needs to have a strong memory that can gather
together all of the accomplishments of his or her trajectory
through the media of artistic expression. There is often a tendency to denigrate past products simply because their conditions of
origin have moved on. But a memory of their potencies can be
retained if a certain mindfulness can be achieved by the genius as
he or she ruminates on the traits and achievements of their past
works of art. One does not have to be in the act of creation to feel
the lasting potency of antecedent works and their internal beauty.
At the same time a certain distance needs to be maintained so
that there is no danger of mere repetition of past aesthetic
choices. The past work can also be reopened in new ways by a
process I have called "emancipatory re-enactment" whereby the
not yet opens out a hidden potency from the past and brings it
forward into the present moment of creativity. For example, a
painter may have briefly used a certain brush technique in one
painting that was not used subsequently. However, in a later work
that same technique was called for but could also take on an even
more radical form and could be emancipated from its past more
circumscribed form. It was re-enacted under new conditions. The
past works, insofar as they are of proper stature, contain many
potencies awaiting the touch of the present creator who can bring
new aesthetic horizons into being for the awaiting community of
interpreters.

The genius, then, must always push forward and produce a
constant and consistently high quality body of work that is available to the larger community, not to mention the artistic community itself. The artistic life, as envisioned by Rank, is one that adds
self-creation to artistic creation, although Rank seems to want
self-creation to replace art itself, the current perspective sees the
artist as paradigmatic for *both* types of creation. In adding a con-

crete body of work to the community the genius also adds to the available stock of beauty in culture and in nature as acculturated. In self-formation the artist is a living experiment in selving on the edges of our horizons and thus an exemplar of the encounter with the sublime.

The saint or the sage is not driven to produce works of beauty that become public artifacts. The story of Thomas Aquinas is profoundly instructive. As a genius he wrote one of the great works in the history of theology and it entered into a vital community of interpreters in Paris in the thirteenth century. However, before completing it he had a mystical vision and abruptly stopped writing, stating that his work on the *Summa* was little more than straw. The saint had replaced the genius in one and the same person. As saint he had no need to build his self through external artistic means. His journey was complete and nothing more was required—the pressure to create was released in one vivid transformation, leaving the artist of thought far behind. The saint had become the *not yet* in the present and time was stilled into the eternal now.

This is not to say that the saint is beyond all struggles, far from it, but it is to say that the inner fire of the genius to create external works is replaced with a drive to manifest the fullness of the godhead. Note that godhead (*die Gottheit*) is not a god or goddess but is the abyss that devours all divinities. The saint overcomes all false gods and sees their relative status as products of the imagination. The genius shares this deconstructive moment with the saint but can still 'use' gods and goddesses in works of art as symbols of important human traits. Unlike the saint the genius can use irony and mythology to give shape to the innumerable divinities cooked up by the fertile species imagination. More often than not, the saint has had a private, that is tribal, revelation that is limited to his or her own tribe or group. Hence the scope of the vision is limited to time and place. For the genius there are many realities and many of them can make their appearance in works of art but always in a non-literal way.

The current perspective gives pride of place to the genius and its world of artistic creation because of the ongoing potency that great works of art have across millennia and diverse cultures. While I might find it almost impossible to enter into a saint's tribal revelation, I can usually gain access to a genius' art work, even if I might need a little instruction in art history—the point is that works of art, on the highest level, are deeply universal and human products that have a built-in drive to help us with our selving process. I can assimilate and manipulate the work of art at my own pace and in my own way. The community of interpreters gives me hermeneutic tools by which to enrich and strengthen my participation in art objects from diverse periods and genre. The worlds that art works can bring me are filled with unending semiotic content and the flow of novel interpretants never flags or grows dim. I can remake myself over and over again and take the artist as my model of selving at its best; namely, as the process of negotiating among the symbolic forms of culture and within the beauties of nature. Ultimately it is the model of the genius on the edge of the Encompassing, open to the sublime, which shapes the trajectory of what it means to be most fully human.

SELECTED BIBLIOGRAPHY

This bibliography follows the style sheet of the Semiotic Society of America, which is based on the historical method of citation. The date following the author's name is the date of the original publication in the original language. The page number to the right is, however, to the translation or edition actually used as noted in the bibliography. For example, the citation (Rank 1930: 113) refers to the 1930 German text, whereas the page number of 113 refers to the English translation as quoted in the text. The advantage of this historical approach is that is keeps texts tied to their moment of origin and reinforces the contextuality of scholarly sources.

ABROMEIT, John, and COBB, Mark W. eds.

2004. *Herbert Marcuse: A Critical Reader*, London: Routledge.

AMERICAN JOURNAL OF THEOLOGY AND PHILOSOPHY.

2013. Special issue on Ecstatic Naturalism, Vol. 34, No. 1.

ATWELL, John.

1995. *Schopenhauer on the Character of the World: The Metaphysics of the Will*, Berkeley: University of California Press.

BADHAM, Paul.

2001. Review of *A Semiotic Theory of Theology and Philosophy*, *Theology*, September–October.

BADHAM, Roger A.

1996. Review of *Nature's Self*, *Critical Review of Books in Religion*, pp. 360–365.
1999. "Windows on the Ecstatic: Reflections on Robert Corrington's Naturalism's," *Soundings*, Vol. 82, No. 3–4, pp. 357–381.

BLOCH, Ernst.

1959. *Das Prinzip Hoffnung*, Frankfurt am Main: Suhrkamp Verlag. English translation, *The Principle of Hope* in three volumes, by Neville Plaice, Stephen Plaice, and Paul Knight, Cambridge, MA: MIT Press, 1986.

BOUVERESSE, Jacques.

1991 (French text). *Wittgenstein Reads Freud: The Myth of the Unconscious*, trans. Carol Cosman, Princeton: Princeton University Press, 1995.

BRENT, Joseph.

1998. *Charles Sanders Peirce: A Life, Revised and Enlarged Edition*, Bloomington: Indiana University Press.

BUCHLER, Justus.

1939. *Charles Peirce's Empiricism*, Kegan, Paul, Trench, Trubner & Co. Reprinted by Octagon Books in 1980.
1951. *Toward a General Theory of Human Judgment*, New York: Columbia University Press. Second revised edition in 1979 from Dover Publications.

1955. *Nature and Judgment*, New York: Columbia University Press.

1961. *The Concept of Method*, New York: Columbia University Press.

1966. *Metaphysics of Natural Complexes*, New York: Columbia University Press. Second expanded edition in 1990 from SUNY Press, ed. Wallace, Marsoobian, Corrington.

1969. On a Strain of Arbitrariness in Whitehead's System," *The Journal of Philosophy*, Vol. 66, p. 589. Reprinted in *Explorations in Whitehead's Philosophy*, eds. Lewis S. Ford and George L. Kline, New York: Fordham University Press, 1983, pp. 280–294.

1974. *The Main of Light: On the Concept of Poetry*, Oxford: Oxford University Press.

CAMPBELL, James.

1995. *Understanding John Dewey*, Chicago, IL: Open Court.

CARTWRIGHT, David E.

2010. *Schopenhauer: A Biography*, Cambridge: Cambridge University Press.

CASSIRER, Ernst.

1929. *Philosophie der symbolischen Formen*, Berlin: Bruno Cassirer. English translation, *The Philosophy of Symbolic Forms* in three volumes, trans. Ralph Manheim, New Haven: Yale University Press, 1955.

CONGER, John P.

1988. *Jung & Reich*: *The Body as Shadow*, Berkeley, CA: North Atlantic Books.

CORRINGTON, Robert S.

1979. "Toward a New Foundation for Pluralism in Religion," *Chrysalis*, Vol. 3, pp. 26–42.

1980. "The Experience of Ringing: Meditations on the Later Heidegger," *The Drew Gateway*, Vol. 53, Winter, pp. 31–48.

1981. "The Christhood of Things: Hopkins' Poem The Windhover," *The Drew Gateway*, Vol. 52, Fall, pp. 41–47.

1981a. "Schleiermacher's Phenomenology of Consciousness and Its Relation to His General Ontology," *Church Divinity 1981*, ed. John H. Morgan, Notre Dame: Church Divinity Monograph Series, pp. 24–41.

1982. "Horizonal Hermeneutics and the Actual Infinite," *Graduate Faculty Philosophy Journal*, Vol. 8, Nos. 1 and 2, pp. 36–97.

1984. "A Comparison of Royce's Key Notion of the Community of Interpretation with the Hermeneutics of Gadamer and Heidegger," *Transactions of the C. S. Peirce Society*, Vol. 20, Summer, pp. 279–301.

1985. "Justus Buchler's Ordinal Metaphysics and the Eclipse of Foundationalism," *International Philosophical Quarterly*, Vol. 25, pp. 289–298.

1985a. "Naturalism, Measure, and the Ontological Difference," *The Southern Journal of Philosophy*, Vol. 23, No. 1, Spring, pp. 19–32.

1986. "John William Miller and the Ontology of the Midworld," *Transactions of the C. S. Peirce Society*, Vol. 22, Spring, pp. 165–188.

1986a. "Josiah Royce and the Sign Community," *Semiotics 1985*, ed. John Deely, Lanham, MD: University Press of American, pp. 238–247.

1987. "C. G. Jung and the Archetypal Foundations of Semiosis," *Semiotics 1986*, ed. Jonathan Evans and John Deely, Lanham, MD: University Press of America, pp. 398–405.

1987a. *The Community of Interpreters: On the Hermeneutics of Nature and the Bible in the American Philosophical Tradition*, Macon, GA: Mercer University Press. Second edition with new preface, 1995.

1987b. "Finitude and Transcendence in the Thought of Justus Buchler," *The Southern Journal of Philosophy*, Vol. 25, No. 4, pp. 445–459.

1987c. "Hermeneutics and Psychopathology: Jaspers and Hillman," *Theoretical and Philosophical Psychology*, Vol. 7, No. 2, pp. 70–80.

1987d. "Introduction to John William Miller's 'For Idealism,'" *The Journal of Speculative Philosophy: New Series*, Vol. 1, No. 4, pp. 257–259.

1987e. "Natural Law and Emancipation: Toward a Theonomous Democracy," *Law and Semiotics,* Vol. 1, ed. Roberta Kevelson, New York: Plenum, pp. 159–179.

1987f. *Pragmatism Considers Phenomenology*, co-edited with Thomas Seebohm and Carl R. Hausman, Washington, DC: Center for Advanced Research in Phenomenology and University Press of America. "Through Temporality to Ordinality," pp. 1–35.

1987g. "Royce on Freedom: Reply to Robert Burch," *The Idea of Freedom in American Philosophy*, ed. Donald S. Lee, *Tulane Studies in Philosophy*, Vol. XXXV, New Orleans: Tulane University Press, pp. 31–34.

1987h. "Toward a Transformation of Neoclassical Theism," *International Philosophical Quarterly*, Vol. 27, No. 4, pp. 391–406.

1988. "Being and Faith: *Sein und Zeit* and Luther," *Anglican Theological Review*, Vol. 70, No. 1, pp. 16–31.

1988a. "John William Miller's 'The Owl,'" *Transactions of the C. S. Peirce Society*, Vol. XXIV, No. 3, pp. 395–398.

1988b. "Metaphysics without Foundations: Jaspers Confrontation with Nietzsche," *Dialogos*, Vol. 52, pp. 73–95.

1988c. "Semiosis and the Phenomenon of Worldhood," *Semiotics 1987*, ed. John Deely, Lanham, MD: University Press of America, pp. 383–393.

1989. "Conversation between Justus Buchler and Robert S. Corrington," *The Journal of Speculative Philosophy*: New Series, Vol. 3, No. 4, pp. 261–274.

1989a. "Faith and the Signs of Expectation," *Semiotics 1988*, ed. Terry Prewitt, John Deely, and Karen Haworth, Lanham, MD: University Press of America, pp. 203–209.

1990. "Emerson and the Agricultural Midworld," *Agriculture and Human Values*, Winter, pp. 20–26.

1990a. "Finite Idealism: The Midworld and Its History," *Bucknell Review*, Vol. 34, No. 1, pp. 85–95.

1990b. "Transcendence and the Loss of the Semiotic Self," *Semiotics 1989*, ed. John Deely, Karen Haworth, and Terry Prewitt, Lanham, MD: University Press of America, pp. 339–345.

1991. "The Emancipation of American Philosophy," *APA Newsletter: Blacks in Philosophy*, Vol. 90, No. 3, pp. 23–26 (with a reply by Cornel West).

1991a. "Horizons and Contours: Toward an Ordinal Phenomenology," *Metaphilosophy*, Vol. 22, No. 3, pp. 179–189.

1991b. "Josiah Royce and Communal Semiotics," *The Semiotic Web 1990*, ed. Thomas A. Sebeok and Jean Umiker-Sebeok, Berlin: Mouton de Gruyter, pp. 61–87.

1991c. *Nature's Perspectives: Prospects for Ordinal Metaphysics*, co-edited with Armen Marsoobian and Kathleen Wallace, Albany: SUNY Press, chapter, "Ordinality and the Divine Natures," pp. 347–366.

1991d. "Peirce and the Semiosis of the Holy," *Semiotics 1990*, ed. Haworth, John Deely, and Terry Prewitt, Lanham, MD: University Press of America, pp. 345–353.

1992. "Ecstatic Naturalism and the Transfiguration of the Good," *Empirical Theology: A Handbook*, ed. Randolph Crump Miller, Birmingham, AL: Religious Education Press, pp. 203–221.

1992a. "Hermeneutics and Loyalty," *Frontiers in American Philosophy*, Vol. 1, ed. Robert Burch and Herman Saatkamp, Jr., College Station: Texas A&M University Press, pp. 357–364.

1992b. *Nature and Spirit: An Essay in Ecstatic Naturalism*, New York: Fordham University Press.

1992c. "Peirce's Melancholy," *Semiotics 1992*, ed. John Deely and Terry Prewitt, Lanham, MD: University Press of America, pp. 332–340.

1993. *An Introduction to C. S. Peirce: Philosopher, Semiotician, and Ecstatic Naturalist*, Lanham, MD: Rowman & Littlefield.

1993a. "Beyond Experience: Pragmatism and Nature's God." *American Journal of Theology and Philosophy*, Vol. 14, No. 2, May, pp. 147–160.

1993b. "From World Exegesis to Transcendence: Jaspers' Critique of Nietzsche," *Karl Jaspers: Philosopher among Philosophers*, ed. Wisser and Ehrlich, Wurzburg: Konigshausen & Neumann, pp. 77–87.

1993c. "The Ground of Being and the Return of the Material Maternal," *Newsletter of the North American Tillich Society*, Vol. XIX, No. 3, July, pp. 3–8.

1993d. "Nature's God and the Return of the Material Maternal," *American Journal of Semiotics*, Vol. 10, Nos. 1–2, pp. 115–132.

1993e. "Peirce the Melancholy Prestidigitator," *Semiotica*, Vol. 94, Nos. 1–2, pp. 85–101.

1993f. "Peirce's Abjected Unconscious: A Psychoanalytic Profile," *Semiotics 1992*, ed. John Deely, Lanham, MD: University Press of America, pp. 91–103.

1994. *Ecstatic Naturalism: Signs of the World*, Advances in Semiotics, Bloomington: Indiana University Press.

1995. "Peirce's Abjection of the Maternal," *Semiotics 1993*, ed. Robert S. Corrington and John Deely, New York: Peter Lang, pp. 590–594.

1995a. "Peirce's Ecstatic Naturalism: The Birth of the Divine in Nature," *American Journal of Theology and Philosophy*, Vol. 16, No. 2, May, pp. 173–187.

1996. *Nature's Self: Our Journey from Origin to Spirit*, Lanham, MD: Rowman & Littlefield.

1996a. "A Web as Vast as Nature Itself," *Semiotica*, Vol. 111, Nos. 1–2, July, pp. 103–115.

1997. "Classical American Metaphysics: Retrospect and Prospect," *Philosophy in Experience: American Philosophy in Transmission*, ed. Richard E. Hart and Douglas R. Anderson, New York: Fordham University Press, pp. 260–281.

1997a. *Nature's Religion*, Lanham, MD: Rowman & Littlefield.

1997b. "Neville's 'Naturalism' and the Location of God," *American Journal of Theology and Philosophy*, Vol. 18, No. 3, September, pp. 257–280.

1997c. "Regnant Signs: The Semiosis of Liturgy," *Semiotica*, Vol. 117, No. 1, pp. 19–42.

1997d. "Taoism and Ecstatic Naturalism," *CKTS Newsletter*, Center of Korean Theological Studies at Drew University, September, p. 1.

1997e. "A Unitarian Universalist Theology for the Twenty-First Century," *Unitarian Universalist Voice*, Vol. 3. No. 3, Fall, pp. 1–9.

1998. "Empirical Theology and its Divergence from Process Thought, *An Introduction to Christian Theology: Contemporary North American Perspectives*, ed. Roger A. Badham, Louisville, KY: Westminster/John Knox.

2000. "Be-Ness and Nothingness in the Secret Doctrine," *The Theosophist*, Vol. 123, No. 8, May, pp. 302–306.

2000a. "Framing and Unveiling in the Emergence of the Three Orders of Value," *The American Journal of Theology and Philosophy*, Vol. 23, No. 1, January, pp. 52–61.

2000b. *A Semiotic Theory of Theology and Philosophy*, Cambridge: Cambridge University Press.

2000c. "World Making, World Taking: The Artifactual Basis of Worldhood," *Semiotica*, Vol. 131, No. 3/4, pp. 229–243.

2003. "Altruism First and Last," *Daily News Bulletin of the 128th International Convention of the Theosophical Society*, Adyar, Chennai, India, No. 4, December, pp. 3–5.

2003a. "Ecstatic Naturalism," *Research News & Opportunities in Science and Theology*, Vol. 3, No. 10, June, p. 1.

2003b. "Jaspers and the Axial Transfiguration of History," *Jaspers on Philosophy and History of Philosophy*, ed. Joseph W. Koterski, S. J. and Ray Langley, Amherst, NY: Humanities Press, pp. 295–302.

2003c. "Karma: Reincarnation and Freedom," *The Theosophist*, Vol. 124, No. 11, August, pp. 414–420.

2003d. "My Passage from Panentheism to Pantheism," *The American Journal of Theology and Philosophy*, Vol. 23, No. 2, May, pp. 129–153.

2003e. *Riding the Windhorse: Manic Depressive Disorder and the Quest for Wholeness*, Lanham, MD: Hamilton Books.

2003f. "Unfolding/Enfolding: The Categorical Schema," *Semiotics 2002*, ed. Terry J. Hewitt and John Deely, New York: Legas, pp. 164–70.

2003g. *Wilhelm Reich: Psychoanalyst and Radical Naturalist*, New York: Farrar, Straus, and Giroux.

2004. "From the Process Self to the Ecstatic Self: Pantheism Reconsidered," *Whitehead, Religion, Psychology*, the Whitehead Society of Korea, pp. 98–05.

2004a. "Infinitizing Psychoanalysis," Proceedings of the Korean Lacan Society, pp. 23–40.

2005. "Response to my Critics," *American Journal of Theology and Philosophy*, Vol. 26, No. 3, September, p. 263.

2005a. "Spinoza, Baruch (1632–1677)," and "Unitarianism," *Encyclopedia of Religion and Nature,* Vol. 2, ed. Bron R. Taylor, New York: Continuum, pp. 1588–1590, 1678–1680.

2006. "American Transcendentalism's Erotic Aquatecture," *Towards a Theology of Eros*, ed. Virginia Burrus and Catherine Keller, New York: Fordham University Press, pp. 221–233.

2007. "Deep Pantheism," *Journal for the Study of Religion, Nature, and Culture*, Vol. 1, No. 4, October, pp. 503–507.

2008. "Cosmology," and "Josiah Royce: Epistemology," *American Philosophy: An Encyclopedia*, ed. John Lachs and Robert Talisse, New York: Routledge, pp. 140–143, 678–679.

2010. "Evolution, Religion, and an Ecstatic Naturalism," *American Journal of Theology and Philosophy,* Vol. 31. Spring, pp. 124–135.

COSTELLOE, Timothy M.

2012. *The Sublime: From Antiquity to the Present*, Cambridge: Cambridge University Press.

CROSBY, Donald A.

2002. *A Religion of Nature*, Albany: SUNY Press.
2009. *Living with Ambiguity: Religious Naturalism and the Menace of Evil*, Albany: SUNY Press.
2011. *Faith and Reason: Their Roles in Religious and Secular Life*, Albany: SUNY Press.

CRUZ, Eduardo.

1995. Review of *Nature and Spirit, The Center for Theory and Natural Sciences Bulletin*, Vol. 15, No. 4, pp. 17–19.

DALTON, Thomas C.

2002. *Becoming John Dewey: Dilemmas of a Philosopher and Naturalist*, Bloomington: Indiana University Press.

DE MARZIO, Darryl.

1997. "Robert Corrington and the Philosophy for Children Program: Communities of Interpretation and Communities of Inquiry," MA Thesis Montclair State University.

DEWEY, John.

1896. "The Reflex Arc Concept in Psychology," Vol. 5, *The Early Works, 1895–1898*, pp. 96–109.
1916. *Democracy and Education*, Vol. 9, *The Middle Works*, Carbondale: Southern Illinois University Press.
1920. *Reconstruction in Philosophy and Essays, The Middle Works*, Carbondale: Southern Illinois University Press.
1925. *Experience and Nature,* Vol. 1, *The Later Works*, Carbondale: Southern Illinois University Press.
1929. *The Quest for Certainty*, Vol. 4, *The Later Works*, Carbondale: Southern Illinois University Press.
1934. *Art as Experience*, Vol. 10, *The Later Works*, Carbondale: Southern Illinois University Press.
1938. *Logic: The Theory of Inquiry*, Vol. 12, *The Later Works*, Carbondale: Southern Illinois University Press.

DRISKILL, Todd A.

1994. "Beyond the Text: Ecstatic Naturalism and American Pragmatism," *American Journal of Theology and Philosophy*, Vol. 15, No. 3, pp. 305–325.

EMERSON, Ralph Waldo.

1983. *Emerson: Essays and Lectures*, New York: Library of America.
1994. *Emerson: Collected Poems and Translations,* New York: Library of America.

FEIERMAN, Jay R.

2009. *The Biology of Religious Behavior: The Evolutionary Origins of Faith and Religion*, New York: Praeger.

FEUERBACH, Ludwig.

1841. *Das Wesen des Christentums.* English translation from second edition (1843), *The Essence of Christianity*, George Eliot, Buffalo, NY: Prometheus Books, 1989.

FRANKENBERRY, Nancy.

1998. Review of *Nature's Self*, *Journal of the American Academy of Religion*, Vol. 66, No. 1, pp. 171–173.

FREUD, Sigmund.

1966. *The Standard Edition of the Complete Psychological Works of Sigmund Freud* in 24 volumes, translated by James Strachey, London: Hogarth Press.

GALE, Richard M.

2010. *John Dewey's Quest for Unity: The Journey of a Promethean Mystic*, Amherst, NY: Prometheus Books.

GRODZINS, Dean.

2002. *American Heretic: Theodore Parker and Transcendentalism*, Chapel Hill: University of North Carolina Press.

GUDMARSDOTTIR, Sigridur.

2005. "Corrington (1950–)," *Encyclopedia of Religion and Nature*, New York: Continuum, p. 420.

GURA, Philip F.

2007. *American Transcendentalism: A History*, New York: Hill and Wang.

HARDWICK, Charley D.

1996. *Events of Grace: Naturalism, Existentialism, and Theology*, Cambridge: Cambridge University Press.

2005. "Worldhood, Betweenness, Melancholy, and Ecstasy: An Engagement with Robert Corrington's Ecstatic Naturalism," *American Journal of Theology and Philosophy*, Vol. 26, No. 3, p. 238.

2006. "Metaphysical Priority and Physicalist Naturalism in Robert Corrington's Ordinal Metaphysics," *American Journal of Theology and Philosophy*, Vol. 27, No. 2–3, pp. 124–214.

HEIDEGGER, Martin.

1927. *Die Grundprobleme der Phänomenologie*. English translation, *The Basic Problems of Phenomenology*, by Albert Hofstadter, Bloomington: Indiana University Press, 1982.

1927a. *Sein und Zeit*. English translation, *Being and Time* by Stambaugh and Schmidt, Albany: SUNY Press, 2010.

1929. *Kant und das Problem der Metaphysik*, Frankfurt. English translation, *Kant and the Problem of Metaphysics*, fourth edition, Richard Taft, Bloomington: Indiana University Press, 1990.

1938/1939. *Bessinung*. English translation, *Mindfulness*, by Emad and Kalary, New York: Continuum.

HUSSERL, Edmund.

1900. *Logische Untersuchungen.* English translation, *Logical Investigations,* in two volumes, by J. N. Findlay with an introduction by Kah Kyung Cho, Amherst, NY: Humanities Books, 2000.
1907. *Die Idee der Phänomenologie.* English translation, *The Idea of Phenomenology,* Alston and Naknikian, Dordrecht, The Netherlands: Kluwer Academic Publishers, 2000.
1913. *Ideen zu einer reinen Phänomenologie und phänomenologischen Philosophie,* Vol. 1, English translation, *Ideas Pertaining to a Pure Phenomenological Philosophy: First Book: General Introduction to a Pure Phenomenology,* by F. Kersten, Dordrecht, The Netherlands: Kluwer Academic Publishers, 1983.
1999. *The Essential Husserl,* ed. Donn Welton, Bloomington: Indiana University Press.

JACQUETTE, Dale, Ed.

1996. *Schopenhauer, Philosophy, and the Arts,* Cambridge: Cambridge University Press.

JAMES, William.

1907. *Pragmatism,* Indianapolis, IN: Hackett, 1981.

JASPERS, Karl.

1935. *Vernuft und Existenz,* Groningen: J. B. Walters. English translation, *Reason and Existence,* by William Earle, New York: Noonday Press, 1955.
1962. *Die philosophischer Glaube angesichts der Offenbarung,* Hamburg: R. Piper & Co., Verlag. English translation, *Philosophical Faith and Revelation,* by E. B. Ashton, New York: Harper & Row, 1967.

JOYCE, James.

1916. *A Portrait of the Artist as a Young Man,* New York: Penguin, 1976.

JUNG, C. G.

1957–1979. *The Collected Works of C. G. Jung* in 20 volumes plus supplements, translated by R. F. C. Hull, Bollingen Series XX, Princeton: Princeton University Press.

KANT, Immanuel.

1781. *Kritik der reinen Vernunft*, Riga, second edition 1787. English translation, *Critique of Pure Reason*, by Paul Guyer and Allen W. Wood, Cambridge: Cambridge University Press, 1998.

1793. *Kritik der Urteilskraft*. English translation, *Critique of the Power of Judgment*, Paul Guyer and Eric Matthews, Cambridge: Cambridge University Press, 2000.

1793a. *Die Religion innerhalb der Grenzen der blossen Vernuft*. English translation, *Reason within the Boundaries of Mere Reason*, by George di Giovanni, *Religion and Rational Theology*, ed. Allen W. Wood and George Di Giovanni, Cambridge: Cambridge University Press, 1996.

KENNETT, Stephen A.

1991. Review of *The Community of Interpreters*, *SAAP Newsletter*, Vol. 59, pp. 15–16.

KIM, Jean.

1999. "Chaos and Order in Nature/Creation," *The Journal of Faith and Science Exchange,* Vol. 3, pp. 193–203.

2003. "Unbearable Fire and Water: The Search for the Spirit of Women in the Discussion of Paul Tillich's 'Spiritual Presence' and Robert S. Corrington's 'Spirit's Eros,'" *Feminist Theology Review*, No. 3, March, pp. 121–144.

KOHUT, Heinz.

1971. *The Analysis of the Self*, Chicago: University of Chicago Press, 2009.

1977. *The Restoration of the Self*, Chicago: University of Chicago Press, 2009.

KRISTEVA, Julia.

1974. *La Révolution du langage poétique*, Paris: Editions du Seuil. English translation, *Revolution in Poetic Language*, by Margaret Waller, New York: Columbia University Press, 1984.
1991. *Etrangers à nous-mèmes*, Librarie Arthème Fayard. English translation, *Strangers to Ourselves*, by Leon S. Roudiez, New York: Columbia University Press, 1991.

LIEBERMAN, James E.

1985. *Acts of Will: The Life and Work of Otto Rank*, New York: The Free Press.
2012. Ed. with Robert Kramer, *The Letters of Sigmund Freud & Otto Rank: Inside Psychoanalysis*, Baltimore: Johns Hopkins University Press.

LOVELY, Edward W.

2012. *George Santayana's Philosophy of Religion: His Roman Catholic Influences and Phenomenology,* with foreword by Robert S. Corrington, Lanham, MD: Lexington Books.

MARCUSE, Herbert.

1956. *Eros and Civilization: A Philosophical Inquiry into Freud*, London: Routledge, 1998.
1964. *One-Dimensional Man: Studies in the Ideology of Advanced Industrial Society*, Boston, MA: Beacon Press, 1991.
1977. *Die Permanenz Der Kunst: Wider eine bestimmte Marxistische Aesthetik*, Munich: Carl Hanser Verlag. English translation, *The Aesthetic Dimension: Toward a Critique of Marxist Aesthetics*, Boston, MA: Beacon Press, 1978.
2007. *Herbert Marcuse: Art and Liberation: Collected Papers, Volume Four*, ed. Douglas Kellner, London: Routledge.

MARION, Jean Luc.

1997. *Etant donné: Essai d'une phénoménologie de la donation*, Presses Universitaires de Frances. English translation, *Being Given: Toward a Phenomenology of Givenness*, by Jeffrey L. Kosky, Stanford: Stanford University Press, 2002.

MARTIN, Jay.

2002. *The Education of John Dewey*, New York: Columbia University Press.

MULLER, Joseph P., and BRENT, Joseph, eds.

2000. *Peirce, Semiotics, and Psychoanalysis*, Baltimore: Johns Hopkins University Press.

NEVILLE, Robert C.

1968. *God the Creator: On the Transcendence and Presence of God*, Chicago: University of Chicago Press. Reprinted with a new preface by SUNY Press, 1992.

1974. *The Cosmology of Freedom*, New Haven: Yale University Press. Reprinted with a new preface by SUNY Press in 1995.

1980. *Creativity and God: A Challenge to Process Theology*, New York: Seabury Press. Reprinted with a new preface by SUNY Press, 1995.

1989. *Recovery of the Measure: Interpretation and Nature*, Albany: SUNY Press.

1991. *A Theology Primer*, Albany: SUNY Press.

1994. Review of *Nature and Spirit* in *International Philosophical Quarterly*, Vol. 34, No. 4, pp. 504–505.

1995. *Normative Cultures*, Albany: SUNY Press.

1996. *The Truth of Broken Symbols*, Albany: SUNY Press.

2000. *Boston Confucianism: Portable Tradition in the Late-Modern World*, with TU Weiming, Albany: SUNY Press.

2005. "Comments on Nature's Religion and Robert Corrington's Aesthetic Naturalism," *American Journal of Theology and Philosophy*, Vol. 26, No. 3.

2006. *On the Scope and Truth of Theology: Theology as Symbolic Engagement*, New York: T&T Clark.

2009. *Ritual and Deference: Extending Chinese Philosophy in a Comparative Context*, Albany: SUNY Press.

2010. *Realism in Religion: A Pragmatist's Perspective*, Albany: SUNY Press.

NGUYEN, Nam T.

2011. *Nature's Primal Self: Peirce, Jaspers, and Corrington*, foreword by Robert S. Corrington, Lanham, MD: Lexington Books.

NIEMOCZYNSKI, Leon J.

2009. "Phenomenology in the American Vein: Justus Buchler's Ordinal Natural-ism and Its Importance for the Justification of Epistemic Objects," *Spontaneous Generations: A Journal for the History and Philosophy of Science*, Vol. 3, No. 1, pp. 9–27.

2011. *Charles Sanders Peirce and a Religious Metaphysics of Nature*, Lanham, MD: Lexington Books.

2013. "Nature's Transcendental Creativity: Deleuze, Corrington, and an Aesthetic Phenomenology," *American Journal of Theology and Philosophy*, Vol. 34, No. 1, pp. 17–34.

PACKER, Barbara L.

2007. *The Transcendentalists*, Athens: University of Georgia Press.

PEIRCE, Charles S.

1898. *Reasoning and the Logic of Things: The Cambridge Conference Lectures of 1898*, ed. Kenneth Laine Ketner, Cambridge: Harvard University Press, 1992.

1903. *Pragmatism as a Principle and Method of Right Thinking: The Harvard Lectures on Pragmatism*, ed. Patricia Ann Turrisi, Albany: SUNY Press, 1997.

1992. *The Essential Peirce: Volume One* (1867–1893), Bloomington: Indiana University Press.

1998. *The Essential Peirce: Volume Two* (1893–1913), Bloomington: Indiana University Press.

PETTIT, Joseph.

2000. Review of *Nature's Religion*, *The Journal of Religion*, Vol. 80, No. 1, pp. 149–151.

POPP, Jerome A.

2007. *Evolution's First Philosopher: John Dewey and the Continuity of Nature*, Albany: SUNY Press.

RAMAL, Randy.

2000. Review of *Nature and Spirit, Ecstatic Naturalism, Nature's Self, and Nature's Religion, Process Studies,* Vol. 21, No. 9, pp. 183–185.

RANK, Otto.

1924 (German Edition). *The Trauma of Birth,* introduction by E. James Lieberman, New York: Dover Publications, 1993.
1930 (German Edition). *Art and Artist: Creative Urge and Personality Development* with a foreword by Anaïs Nin, translated by Charles Francis Atkinson, New York: W.W. Norton, 1968.

RAPOSA, Michael L.

1989. *Peirce's Philosophy of Religion,* Bloomington: Indiana University Press.
2002. Review of *A Semiotic Theory of Theology and Philosophy, Modern Theology,* Vol. 18, No. 2, pp. 302–304.

REICH, Wilhelm.

1927. *Die Entdeckung des Orgons, Erster Teil: Die Function des Orgasmus.* English translation by Vincent R. Carfagno, *The Function of the Orgasm: Sex-Economic Problems of Biological Energy,* 1973, New York: Farrar, Straus, and Giroux.
1933. *Charakteranalyse.* English translation of third expanded edition by Vincent R. Carfagno, *Character Analysis,* 1972, New York: Farrar, Straus, and Giroux.
1933a. *Die Massenpsychologie des Faschismus.* English translation by Vincent R. Carfagno, *The Mass Psychology of Fascism,* 1970, New York: Farrar, Straus, and Giroux. Expanded edition 1942.
1946. *Rede an den kleinen Mann.* English translation by Ralph Manheim with illustrations by William Steig, *Listen Little Man!* 1974, New York: Farrar, Straus, and Giroux.
1951. *Ether, God and Devil* and *Cosmic Superimposition,* New York: Farrar, Straus, and Giroux. Translation of added sections in 1971 by Therese Pol.

RYAN, Alan.

1995. *John Dewey and the High Tide of American Liberalism,* New York: W.W. Norton.

SAFRANSKI, Rudiger.

1990. *Schopenhauer and the Wild Years of Philosophy*, Cambridge: Harvard University Press.

SANTAYANA, George.

1905. *The Life of Reason*, New York: Charles Scribner.
1923. *Scepticism and Animal Faith*, New York: Charles Scribner.
1925. "Dewey's Naturalistic Metaphysics," *Journal of Philosophy*, Vol. 22, No. 25, reprinted in *Dewey and His Critics*, ed. S. Morgenbesser, New York: *The Journal of Philosophy*, pp. 343–358.
1942. *The Realms of Being*, New York: Charles Scribner.

SCHELLING, F. W. J.

1809. *Über das Wesen der menschlichen Freiheit*, Stuttgart: Reclam. English translation, *Philosophical Investigations into the Essence of Human Freedom*, by Jeff Love and Johannes Schmidt, Albany: SUNY Press, 2007.

SCHLEIERMACHER, Friedrich.

1799. *Über die Religion: Reden an die Gebildetenunter ihren Verhtern*, Berlin. English translation, *On Religion: Speeches to its Cultured Despisers*, Richard Crouter, Cambridge: Cambridge University Press, 1988.
1821. *Die Glaubenslehre*, Berlin. English translation of second edition, *The Christian Faith,* H. R. Mackintosh and J. S. Stewart, Philadelphia: Fortress, 1999.

SCHOPENHAUER, Arthur.

1819. *Die Welt als Wille und Vorstellung*, Leipzig. English translation, *The World as Will and Presentation,* Vol. 1, by Richard E. Aquila and David Carus, New York: Pearson Longman, 2008.
1841. *Die Beiden Grundprobleme der Ethik*. English translation, *The Two Fundamental Problems of Ethics,* by Christopher Janaway, Cambridge: Cambridge University Press, 2009.

SHARP, Douglas.

1990. Review of *The Community of Interpreters*, *Church History*, Vol. 59, No. 4, pp. 592–594.

SIEGEL, Allen M.

1996. *Heinz Kohut and the Psychology of the Self*, London: Routledge.

SINGER, Beth J.

1983. *Ordinal Naturalism: An Introduction to the Philosophy of Justus Buchler*, Lewisburg: Bucknell University Press.

SONESON, Jerome Paul.

1993. *Pragmatism and Pluralism*, Minneapolis, MN: Fortress Press.

SPIEGELBERG, Herbert.

1982. *The Phenomenological Movement: A Historical Movement, Third Revised and Enlarged Edition*, The Hague: Martinus Nijhoff Publishers.

SRI AUROBINDO.

1940. *The Life Divine*, Twin Lakes, WI: Lotus Press, 1990.

STONE, Jerome A.

2008. "Other Current Religious Naturalists: Robert Corrington," *Religious Naturalism Today: The Rebirth of a Forgotten Alternative*, Albany: SUNY Press, pp. 211–219.

TILLICH, Paul.

1912. *Mystik and Shuldbewusstein in Schelling's philosophischer Entwicklung*, Berlin. English translation, *Mysticism and Guilt-Consciousness in Schelling's*

Philosophical Development, by Victor Nuovo, Lewisburg: Bucknell University Press, 1974.

1919. "Über die Idee einer Theologie der Kultur," *Religionsphilosophie der Kultur*, Berlin. English translation, "On the Idea of a Theology of Culture," in *What Is Religion?* by James Luther Adams, New York: Harper Torchbooks, 1969.

1933. *Die sozialistische Entscheidung*, Alfred Prottle, Potsdam. English translation, *The Socialist Decision*, by Franklin Sherman, New York: Harper & Row, 1977.

1951. *Systematic Theology*, Vol. I, Chicago: University of Chicago Press.

1952. *The Courage to Be*, New Haven: Yale University Press.

1957. *Systematic Theology*, Vol. II, Chicago: University of Chicago Press.

1963. *Systematic Theology*, Vol. III, Chicago: University of Chicago Press.

WARD, Roger.

2001. Review of *A Semiotic Theory of Theology and Philosophy*, *Philosophy in Review*, Vol. 21, No. 6, pp. 411–413.

2004. "Robert Corrington and the Transformation of Consciousness," *Conversion in American Philosophy: Exploring the Process of Transformation*, New York: Fordham University Press, pp. 203–216.

WESTBROOK, Robert B.

1991. *John Dewey and American Democracy*, Ithaca: Cornell University Press.

WICKS, Robert.

2008. *Schopenhauer*, Oxford: Blackwell.

WILDMAN, Wesley J.

2002. Review of *A Semiotic Theory of Theology and Philosophy*, *The Journal of Religion*, Vol. 82, No. 4, pp. 657–658.

WOODWARD, Guy.

1997. "Cleaving the Light: The Necessity of Metaphysics in the Practice of Theology," MA Thesis, Loras College.

INDEX

ABOUT THE AUTHOR

Robert S. Corrington is professor of philosophical theology in the graduate division of religion at Drew University in Madison, New Jersey. He has published nine previous books as an ongoing project of creating and expanding the philosophical and theological perspective of his ecstatic naturalism. From the beginning his work has been concerned with bringing classical American philosophy into dialogue with Continental thought. Just as important is his commitment to post-Freudian psychoanalysis and its correlation to semiotics and metaphysics. He has served on the Boards of the Semiotic Society of America and the Highlands Institute and as president of the Karl Jaspers Society of North America.

Beauty - Kant → Introspection, Wicksay Exp?
Sobline - Jaspers - shipwreck → Introspection
Tragic — Ethical Category   ✓ Sometimes
           ↳ Schopenhaung Mitleid   "Committed
                                        art"
     ↓   ↓
           Inhtrospection

Appeal.

― Selvms + Mitleid → Relationship?
              ↳ is I Vicarious introspection?
                        ↳ Wikle calls it empaty
                                    → converts schopenhaues

― Kohut's Vicarious introspection
     use of mitleid
  → 2 N → Moral Awareness
  → Equate Suffering w Morally Reprehensible schopenhaue
              ↳ Use source "we" to convert schopenhaue
                    of the "we" → Rescues hm from a sagsin (N+S
Mitleid → The Embodying   EU.'s committed to 3 A
AS. → Metaphorical Ethics   =   EU.'s committed to 3 A
  Kohut → Plato + Psyco - Ethics

& See till tick 38 loss of meaning
                    ↳ Double anxiety of
                 comparison + knowing
                 that it is meaningless
                 + empty arguing

[it Regues
 Imagination

P.2 is AS. sympathy of pleasure?

87. Phenomenology + Metaphysics

142. AS. will to Life + Nature Noting

148. AS. on Art

151 How does Art Relate to Ethics?

152 AS. Art + Solving

1" Role of Art

153 Marcuse + Political Art

154 Art struggles toward the Universal

157 Peirce aesthetics foundational for Ethics — Normative discipline.

158 Art + sublime

169 — The Moral Life

171 — Is shipwreck required?
    ↳ sublime → finite → Infinite
       beauty finite → finite

175 — post Religious space Aesthetic
       to Encounter the Art
          ↳ Traits of sublime

176 — Work of Art cues for beauty + sublime

180 — Comedy locus of experience of the sublime
       ↳ excepting conditions of Jester

181 = 182 social sublime ✗ → Define — Ethical social sublime?

_____

1. Ethical Potency of Art | 114 Empathetic Phenomenology
                                  | 137 Method is the foundation
29 — Solving | of Ethics
39 — Natural Empathy |
03 Method |

Eth –ethics
a/ recreation

(Psyche + The Moral Aesthetic:
An opening foray into an Ethos
of En

- Empathetic role the
  psyche will play u talke
  Ethos
- Humans unique in ethos debate